Born To Be Healthy and Thin!!!

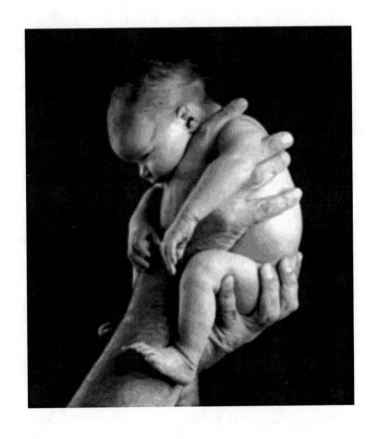

Steven A. Komadina, M.D.

An Owner's Manual For Your Body

The author does not intend this book to be a substitute for advice from your own medical or health professional who has examined you and knows your physiology and lab tests.

You should consult them before you proceed with any recommendations in *Born to Be Healthy and Thin.*

Anyone with a known disease or serious health condition or who is taking over the counter or prescription medications, should especially check with their personal physician or health practitioner before changing or discontinuing the dosage of medications or supplements.

You may want to discuss the material presented here with them, so that they can assist you in making any changes based on the information presented here.

Dr. Komadina and the publishers specifically disclaim any responsibility for adverse health effects occurring because of personal application or the use of the information presented in this book.

This book, like most things in life, is 90% opinion and perhaps 10% fact. It's main purpose is to stimulate you to question and ponder your body and the "opinions" about it you have been taught in the past.

You must find your own personal "facts".

To my parents
Tony and Marjorie Komadina
who gave me my DNA and
encouraged me to question and study life

and

to my six children
Jennifer, Amy, Rebecca, Spencer,
Neal and Mark

and

their children

For Receiving the Family DNA
And Passing It On!

May they also have lifetimes
filled with the search for further
light and knowledge.

May "Life's Force" be with them!

Acknowledgements

If there has ever been a life full of influential people, it surely has been mine. I have been blessed with people who have given their time to educate, inspire, and motivate. What I have accomplished could not have been done without them. In many cases others have worked harder than I did, while I received the applause on stage.

My daughter Amy Victor, is certainly one of those. She fills in the gaps, dots the "I"s, crosses the "T"s and works endlessly to make me look good and succeed. No amount of thanks will ever repay her for her loyalty and dedication to "Dad."

This book represents a lifetime of seeking to understand the human body and the workings of this marvelous physical temple for my spirit. There have been authors and speakers who have truly blazed the trail for my quest for understanding and knowledge.

Chief among them are Michael R. Eades, M.D. and Mary Dan Eades, M.D. Their series of books are outstanding and I recommend *The Protein Power* series to all my patients. Barry Sears and his *Zone* series further confirmed my beliefs.

Dr. Mercola added even more confirmation that we were on the right path to wellness, vitality and true understanding of what our body needs to live it's destiny of health, wellness and permanent optimal weight.

Jamie McManus, M.D. shared her stage with me in countless cities and proved to be a mentor when no other "real doctor" would talk to me. She was always available for long talks to confirm my newfound beliefs. When the world of Organized Medicine seemed to discard this new knowledge, she was always there as a safe harbor to reassure and encourage. I will be eternally grateful to her and for her friendship.

My friendship with Jim Rohn, life and business philosopher, helped me to think out of the box and then to feel comfortable out of the box. Jim has wisdom far beyond his 70 + years and I will forever be grateful for his sharing it with me.

Mark Hughes, a kid who succeeded beyond belief, served as an example of correct attitude and willingness to dream, to do more and be more. He taught me to care more about who I become, than what I get in life.

Professor David Heber, M.D. of U.C.L.A. and

Louis Ignaro, PhD, Nobel Prize winner from UCLA, also shared knowledge and made me think and question.

My friends, around the world, who pick me up at airports, check me into hotels, cater to my every need and pack the venues for my talks. None of this would be possible without them.

Chuck Park -- South East Asia
John Purdy – South East Asia
Joseph Wojck – South East Asia
Young-Hee Chung – Korea
Mamie and Trey Herron -- Singapore
Johnny Wang – Taiwan
Jasmine Ma -- Taiwan
Ping Chen -- Taiwan
Gary Huang – Philippines
Mec Umali – Philippines
Lyn Vallejera -- Philippines
Roger Tan – Singapore
Wallapa Narunatvanich -- Thailand
Veena Changpirom --Thailand
Cheewathum Sanittamayuthi -- Thailand
Deddy Aryadi – Indonesia
Ashali Mustaram – Indonesia
Kaori Nishiuchi -- Japan
Neil Spiers – Europe
Florencia Fernandez – Argentina

Marcos Gasser – Argentina
Marcelo Rappaport -- Argentina
James Hopkins – United Kingdom
Mahrukh and Joe Campbell -- Canada
Tony Vendryes, M.D. – Jamaica
Pedro and Juliane Cardoso – Brazil
Tae Ho Kim and Hyun Moo – Korea
Ingrid Wouters -- Belgium
Dominique Wauters --Belgium
Penny and Tony Wing -- United Kingdom
Martinha and Jaime Kosman -- Brazil

Fellow believers in the unlimited potential of
the human body and spirit who are dedication
to health and wellness: Leslie Stanford, Geri
Citanovich, Susan Peterson O'Brian, Dennis
Dowdell, John & Lori Tartol, Kurt & Cindy
O'Connell, Dan Waldren, Alan Lorenz, Markus
Lehmann, Leon Waisbein, Amertat Cohn, Tish
Rochin, John Peterson, Michiko DeJaeghere,
Az & Sharon Ansari, Steffan Gratziani, Doran
& Emiko Andry, Trina & Dante Andry, Jeff &
Kathy Orr, Michael Johnson, Peter Castleman,
Michael & Debi Katz, Paul Michaels, Potato
Richardson, Julie Weaver, John Murphy, Joseph
McClindon III, Suzanne & Cody Morrow, Greco
Garcia, Rosie & Paco Perez, Pam Kingsley,
Judith Kyker, Elizabeth Thomson, Jim & Judy
Jacobson, Sonja & Rich Palmer,

Craig & Carolyn Tsudakowa, Glen & Kellie Hosaka, Steve & Debbie Combs, Marilyn & Charles Combs, Dan & Wendy Caldwell, Dave & Leila Kammerman, Heather & Larry Hulsey, Angela Bujnevicie, Pat & Deborah Boyd, Don & Deanna Williamson, Andrew Coltman, Gary & Dayna Spurgeon, Meg & Paul Lile, Mark Matika, Dava & Allan Buynum, J. & Lisa Curtis, Carol Curtin, Dan Delphia, Beverly Esche, Robert & Julie Ford, Arelene Geraci, Pam & Brad Harris, Clem Herron, Linda & Pat Hursey, Stanislav Kartin, Hal Koppel, Frank Lutz, Linda Arbertino, Cynthia Martin, Jim McCue, Jan & Zane Miller, Blake Morgan, Alexander & Tatiana Naimushina, Masako Muto, Sharon Peterman, Mike and Cindy Patterson, Annette Petrocelli, Rinaldo & Maritza Porcile, Cynthia Robinson, Larry Shine, Leah Singleton, Doug Stuntz, Jim Tartol, Al & Jan Vizina, Larry Ward, Rick Wolter, Mark Zuckerbrod, Irene Sullivan, Linda Campbell, Mark & Natalee Bowen, Jodi & Brad Schmolesky Ron & Renae Steger, Kieth & Tami Porter, Henry Neuman, , Mette Hyldegaard, Doug Smith, Susan Gail, Ellie Folkers and Kim & Dave Edwards.

Joseph Smith, Jr., who gave me the keys to truly understanding why I am here and what I can become. He set an example of courage to defend beliefs and truth that stay with me daily. He seems like a brother and a guide to further light and knowledge I have always desired. His encouragement to question and study and reach within me for the strength to say what I believe, regardless of the consequences, have led to the openness of this book.

And last but certainly not least, my eternal companion Penny, who has shared over 40 years of adventure, and excitement married to a guy who always had a cause, a new passion, and was an eternal questioner of life and all that it entails. One friend even described me as a "fertile mind always looking for a new direction to grow." How I was lucky enough to find her is one of those mysteries of life. I want her to know that without her I could never have accomplished all I have accomplished. She is the great woman behind this man. My imperfections have nothing to do with her, but all my successes have her mark on them.

Steven A. Komadina, M.D., F.A.C.O.G.

Table of Contents

Introduction

Write a book? Does the world really need one more book on wellness, prevention, and nutrition?

That is the question I asked myself for many years as I read everything I could get my hands on. There are lots of great books. I could hardly put them down as I read into the late hours of the night. None of this was information I had learned in medical school in the 60s. Yet it was soooooooo important for me, my family and my patients to know! Why didn't I hear about this sooner?

I tried to discuss what I was discovering with the other doctors in the hospital's doctor's lounge, but they would look at me like I was crazy and quickly change the topic to the more traditional topics like declining reimbursement, loss of control, managed care, recent divorces or the favorite topic…..

THE MALPRACTICE CRISIS!!!!

Then I tried to get my patients and family to read the books. It just never seemed to happen. They were too busy or wanted me to read the book and then give them a book report to save them time. So that is what I have done for the last 6 years, as nutrition has become my passion in life. I have given "book reports" all over the world to willing listeners.

I have shared my thoughts with over a million people worldwide via live lectures, television interviews, magazine articles, legislative committee meetings and DVDs.

I have had frequent requests to make tapes of my talks or for me to send people my notes of talks they have heard. Because of that, I am now convinced that a book is due to share my opinions on the secrets of life, health and vitality. That's right….. MY OPINIONS. You see I am not threatened by admitting I don't know it all. Furthermore, I am also convinced no one else knows it all either.

We live in a planet filled with imperfect people, who share their opinions as though they were facts. A ninth grade dropout, self-made billionaire Mark Hughes, taught me that 90% of what you hear in the world is opinion and 10% is fact. As I have grown older, and I hope wiser, I know he was right. We spend our lives being afraid to admit we don't know something for fear we will be judged as "dumb" or of less worth than others. This fear of making a mistake was drubbed into us in school, where we were constantly being graded on all we did by not only our teachers, but also our friends, family and relatives. Hence we have settled into lives of acting out who we want the world to believe we are, rather than being ourselves.

THIS BOOK IS MY CURRENT OPINION OF WHAT I THINK REPRESENTS FACT!!!!!!

I hope you will find the contents of this book thought provoking, revealing and life changing. Writing this book for me has been all three.

I have an owner's manual for almost everything I own, but I never found an owner's manual accompanying any of the 16,000 + babies I delivered over the last 40 years.

This book is my attempt to create such a manual. It is written for the average "Body Owner" and is not bogged down with meticulous documentation. The documentation exists and more disciplined writers have included that documentation in those books which I have included in my "Recommended Reading List" in Appendix I.

A warning once again to readers that 90% of what you hear or read in the world, even by "experts", is opinion and only 10% is fact. Even highly touted "Evidence Based Medicine" is "opinion" based on the current evidence, which may or may not be correct. It has been estimated that at least 50% of what is taught in medical schools will eventually be found to not be correct! I have spent the last 35 years trying to figure out which 50% to forget. I officially apologize to my patients for my medical school's mistakes caused

by "Evidenced Based Medicine" unwillingness to admit what they teach is "Current Opinion"......
.. Not Fact.

I must thank my parents for instilling within me a burning desire to get all the education that I could. Neither of my parents had the opportunity to get a university degree, but they were determined that I would have such an opportunity. They taught me early in life to learn no matter what I was doing. We had many educational vacations riding free passes on the Santa Fe Railway. My father worked 30 years for the railroad as a yard clerk and announcer of the comings and goings of trains in and out of Albuquerque, New Mexico.

I was encouraged to question anyone and anything and hence the ease with which I accepted the challenge to learn more about the human body than I had learned in traditional medical school. I was encouraged to question. I did so in subsequent postgraduate continuing education courses I attended that were financed and sponsored by pharmaceutical companies. I also attended courses from medical schools that were also financed by pharmaceutical companies.

I was exposed to "ethnic medicine" as I took care

of Native Americans, Spanish American Folk Healers, and Oriental Immigrants. In 1969-1970 I served as a "Clinic Doctor" working out of the back of a Land Rover in the backcountry of Nepal. I sat with Tibetan Monks in their stupas where I administered to their health needs, and worked among bow and arrow hunter-gatherer villagers with no written language in the Chitwan Forest. While lying in my tent at night listening to the sounds of a jungle wide awake as the tiger hunted, I asked myself what I was really doing. How was I to make a difference in the world. Where could I best use my medical talents and philosophical drive to be a giver and not a taker during my life.

Obstetrics allowed me to spend most of my medical life welcoming new spirits to earth. I was a giver. What a miracle that was. It never became boring or routine. Every birth was unique, just like every baby. However, I began to realize as much as every person is unique, we had much in common as well. As I began to deliver second generations, I realized how much I needed to do to insure those babies had quality of life and not a death sentence brought about by heart disease, cancer, stroke and diabetes.

My patients were also looking for the keys

to health. They shared information they had discovered and taught me a great deal. I am so grateful that they shared the alternative treatments and medical philosophies they found. I was a careful observer, and was frequently amazed at what I saw happen as they used these "unproven" techniques and got results! I had to know more about what I saw!

I drove my partners crazy, always wanting to consider trying this or that new approach. Finally I realized I was making them sick by bringing so much uncertainty and desire for change into their lives and our partnerships. That was when 20 + years ago I struck out on my own and began a practice called Women's Health Horizons. That practice eventually evolved into just plain Health Horizons. I must thank past partners, especially John Bennett, for trying to understand and forgive the stress and upheaval I know I caused in their lives with my driven personality and ever-changing ideas for change.

Several times I was seduced by the desire to reach more people and be bigger, with multiple offices. I hired doctors, midwives and nurse practitioners, but they never really could grasp the holistic concept I was trying to create. I wanted a true partnership with patients, where they were actually in control. I was merely their educator and first-aid giver. My patients got the concept and loved it, but loss of control was not comfortable for my fellow practitioners.

Then in 1997, I had a personal health crisis as I reached over 300 pounds while "eating less and exercising more." A new quest had begun. I had learned how to starve patients and myself years earlier, but it stopped working, as my weight continued to go up and down every 3-4 years.

That is when I truly had an epiphany and discovered that only through perfect nutrition, not starvation, could I lose and teach my patients to lose and maintain their ideal weight. I was lucky enough to once again learn from patients and friends that scientists had already figured this out. With a combination of perfect meals in the form of balanced shakes and supplements from Herbalife, I was able to lose 115 pounds in 10 months and have kept my new "shape" ever since.

I was then relentless in my pursuit of why and how nutrition worked and how to help my patients. That has brought me to where I am today. Jetting around the world. Lecturing to doctors and the public on almost every continent. Reaching the world through television interviews and nutrition talks. Now I am writing this book.

I firmly believe what I share with you in this book. The words are still my opinion. I am really impressed that the human body is so complicated and has so many interactions going on at the same time, that simple thoughts like "calories in….. calories out" sound logical, but are naive and have led to the obesity epidemic in the world today. The only thing more naïve is the great American experiment of 40 years of no fat or low fat diet, which once again, has not prevented disease but caused disease.

Unfortunately "we experts" are afraid to admit we have been WRONG! We continually try to justify theories based on incorrect science and "evidenced based mistakes" to prove to the world we are not wrong, when the new evidence shouts for our attention and need to change our theories.

We have experts afraid to be GRADED "F" because of an imperfect education system that has trained us to accept lies as truth to save face.

EVERYDAY THAT MENTALITY IS KILLING THE PEOPLE OF THE WORLD!

This book is an attempt to get you to wakeup and find your own truth. YOU HAVE THE ABILITY, THE INTELLECT, AND THE RIGHT TO FIND YOUR OWN TRUTH.

DO NOT BE AFRAID TO LIVE YOUR LIFE FOR YOU AND NOT FOR YOUR FELLOW BEINGS.

YOU ARE NO LONGER BEING GRADED!

The Eskimo 100 years ago had a diet of 80% fat…… animal and fish fat, and had no heart disease, little cancer, normal blood pressure and no diabetes. So who talked us into low fat? Was that part of the 50% I was taught in medical school that was incorrect?

One of the problems is that once we accept a theory, we close our eyes to evidence that we were wrong. I think the medical profession is afraid to admit they were wrong and it is killing the people of the world everyday as we spread the American or Western Diet around the world. I feel this is an example of intellectual hypocrisy and ignorance.

Maybe it is time to say we were wrong. I am not afraid to say that and hence another reason for this book.

These are the provocative subjects we will address in this book.

It is written so that each chapter almost stands on its own and can be read in any order. Line upon line and precept upon precept works best. Read a little. Contemplate what you have read. Discuss it with family and friends. See what your health practitioner says. Then take responsibility for your own health.

No one cares more about your health than you. Please care about your body and mind. I am convinced you can be whatever and whoever you want to be. Your body wants to live. Your body wants to be healthy. Your body wants to think clearly. Your body wants you to be your optimal weight for your age. This I am sure of.

Look to nature for the answers. I have been doing this all my life. You do not find fat wild animals. Wild animals are either all the same, thin if there is a famine, old or sick. They can eat whenever they want, but they can only eat what they find in nature. No fast food outlets for antelopes, jackrabbits, or coyotes. Are we any different than those mammals? Why do the animals we keep in zoos and as pets develop the same diseases we develop and their wild ancestors do not develop them?

Read on and I promise you will learn what an owner's manual might have included had you come with one at birth. I once again tell you I am not smart enough to write the exact manual. I firmly believe no mortal will ever understand how our body-mind connection works in this life. I don't care if you are a university professor or even won a Nobel prize!

NO ONE ON THE FACE OF THE EARTH UNDERSTANDS THE HUMAN BODY!

We are merely kidding ourselves. All I ask is that we observe what naturally happens if we <u>don't</u> try to improve on nature. The problem is that we have so changed the earth over many generations, that we will never know what we are missing and what our healthy, thin ancestors had to eat every day.

This, however, I firmly believe (remember "opinion")........ our food has changed beyond recognition from our natural diet. ALL humans on the face of the earth must, therefore, supplement for any chance of getting their bodies once again nourished.

<u>REMEMBER:</u>

Nourishment = Life

Poor or Malnutrition = Death

It's that simple.

Steven A. Komadina, M.D.
November 2005

Before
You Were
Born........

This is not a chapter on what happened to you in the womb, but it is a history of your ancestors who gave your DNA to you as a gift. We have no option to choose our parents, but we have total control over what we do with that DNA.

DNA is the heart of our cells. Chromosomes, genes, genome, all are words we have heard in the past. Their exact meaning is not important.

What is important is the understanding that they are what make us unique human beings. They control our physical characteristics. They are responsible for our talents. They are responsible for who we are.

They also begin to change from the first breath we take. The fact is that, we begin to die as soon as we take our first breath. We will discuss this in upcoming chapters.

What we want to understand now is that the original DNA set down tens of thousands of years ago still governs our bodies today. That DNA is responsible for our sickness and our health. You see, the majority of the major illnesses today are a result of an imbalance with our ancient DNA and our modern lifestyle.

This was so exciting as I learned it and began to realize that it was the key to the health of my patients and my family. Why hadn't I learned this in medical school? It was not only logical, but life changing as I realized what it did to my understanding of disease.

What did the dinner table look like 30,000 years ago or more? That was the key question. We ate fruits and vegetables we gathered in the world around us. There was no agriculture back when our DNA formed. We ate what was currently growing and producing in its season. You couldn't eat an apple a day to keep the healer away. They were only ripe in the fall!!! Does that mean we should only eat apples in the fall? Those are the questions I began to ask. Did we need more carbohydrates in the fall to store fat for the long cold winter months? What about our ancestors who lived in the temperate zone where there were fruits and vegetables year around? Did they have a different DNA?

These are very fundamental questions that must be asked. With our advanced brain, we could survive harsh times. We figured out how to regulate our temperature by wearing clothing made from the things around us. We migrated with the animals as the weather changed and the food for the animals we preyed on changed. Man was a predator!! He wasn't strong or fast, but he was smart. He became the ultimate predator because of his brain not his brawn.

We lived in family groups, not in large towns. In fact we did not even live in villages for most of our existence on the face of the earth. Can you now be able to grasp the enormity of the changes we have gone through socially and culturally, but not physiologically?

We have the same DNA that those people had. Five hundred generations is all we are talking about. Mutations do not occur that quickly in nature. We are the SAME, hence the problems with our health and our nutrition. Quite simply we are eating food that is totally artificial and never intended to be eaten by human beings. In fact 95% of all we find in even an organic grocery store today NEVER EXISTED 100 YEARS AGO!!!!!!!

Think about it. Compare a wild strawberry with a store bought strawberry today. If you have never seen a wild strawberry (that is only ripe for several weeks a year) THEY ARE THE SIZE OF A GREEN PEA!!!

What about apples? They were in reality like crab apples of today, not the large Fuji and Delicious apples you find 12 months a year in the modern supermarket.

Melons were small. There were only certain fruits and plants in limited places in the world. No refrigeration, no cold storage, no transportation of food within hours around the world to all climates. No stores. You gathered it and you ate it. No middleman existed until we began to trade with neighboring tribes and families or migrating peoples.

Our diet was high in fat. Usually we lived where animals lived and we found ways to kill them or ate what was left after they ate what they had killed. In primitive campsites around the world, archeologists find broken bones and skulls, which bear testimony that our ancestors ate the marrow in bones as well as the brains of the animals they killed or scavenged. Marrow and brain is FAT!

There is a landmark study done on the aboriginal people of Australia. In a controlled study, a group of aborigines in the city were compared to their relatives who were sent back to the outback. At the end of the study those who had returned to their hunter-gatherer life had less heart disease, cancer, high blood pressure and diabetes than their relatives who all got more disease during the study while living in the city. Of even more interest, was the fact those in the city actually burned more than twice the kilocalories of those in the primitive existence outback. This confirmed other studies that showed our primitive ancestors did NOT live lives filled with arduous physical activity. Much of that activity did not occur until we developed an agricultural life style. Bottom line: our original ancestors did not exercise unless they were running for their lives.

So the challenge is to ask what we as modern humans must do to recapture the health and ability to maintain an optimal weight that occurred universally among our primitive ancestors. Did these people have diseases as we know them today?

I began to even question the meaning of the word "disease." What was a disease given this new understanding? I suddenly realized that most traditional disease was in reality not a disease but a symptom of something going wrong in the body.

I then realized that sickness only occurred in two ways.

1. I would catch something: virus, bacteria, fungus, or parasite.

or

2. Something changed in my body.

"Catch Something"
or
"Something Changes"

You don't catch heart disease. You have something change in your body. So why does change occur?

It could result from an injury. We break a bone. We fall off a cliff. A wild animal gores us. We are injured in a fight with an enemy tribe. We fall through the ice. We stub our toe in the dark. We cut our self on a sharp object. These are all physical injuries.

But what changes us on the inside? Could it be irritation? Perhaps inflammation is the culprit? Perhaps a poison gets in? Something gets in that is not supposed to be there for the health of our body. That something then interferes with our body's function and its repair and regeneration.

What can get inside our body to change it if not something we catch? I can only think of two things.

1. What we breath.

2. What we swallow.

We will examine the number one killer of all living things....... OXYGEN...... in a subsequent chapter.

In reality, it is usually our food that is swallowed, that potentially causes change.

Most species of plants or animals have become extinct because they could not get their food. The climate changed, an epidemic wiped out their food, etc. In America at least today, most illness is associated with food and malnutrition. Are we then a species on the way to extinction? Think about it. I think there is no question that we are. That's my opinion.

Read on. I will try to show you the evidence I used as a basis for my medical opinions. Does this make my opinions "evidenced based medicine"?

nutrition, or in the information in this book. You can change risk, but may have no control over causes. I firmly believe that the information and recommendations contained in this book will decrease the probability of your having dysfunction of your body systems and, thereby, reduce risk for some diseases. I hope it will also increase the probability of you living a long and healthy life.

Remember, medical knowledge is incomplete. No one on earth understands the human body in all its glorious complexity. Recommendations from any doctor are based on a combination of current knowledge, clinical judgment, common sense, and plain old hunches. There is an art to medicine. There is an art to healing. There is no lab test or X-ray for common sense and experience. Outcomes are probabilistic and no one can predict what the outcome will be in any individual case. We as doctors play the odds the best we can.

We win some and we lose some.

Learn to listen to your body and reflect on experiences of the past. Make your own decisions based on your experience with your body. It is your right to use your experience to make health decisions. The probability is that you may be just as lucky as your doctor when he rolls the dice with your health management decisions.

Now is the time
to participate
in your health care!

Origins of Life: Evolution, Intelligent Design or Extraterrestrials....

- Where did we come from?
- Why are we here?
- Where will we go at death?

The eternal questions.......

Ultimately we must find our own answers.

Evolution:

We were all taught it in school. Remember Darwin and the Galapagos Islands? We all learned the concept to pass the test. It seemed logical. It was presented as science and after all, science is about truth....... isn't it?

There are evidences of micro evolution in the world around us. The changing of a beak. The color of a lizard. We can manipulate crops and flowers and even breed dogs and cows and horses for color and size and even disposition.

Are these not examples of evolution? Man's manipulation of genes takes place daily in laboratories seeking to unlock the mysteries of life. Is this what evolution is all about? Mysteries? We can even clone living things today. So doesn't that just prove evolution is how we got here? Or..... is evolution another example of mystery masquerading as fact?

That is for you to decide.

Extraterrestrials:

Now come on!!!! You have got to be kidding. Did we come from outer space? Were our ancestors introduced here from another world? Would that account for the sudden appearance of Homo sapiens and the disappearance of his contemporary the Neanderthal? There is just as much evidence for this origin of life, in reality, as evolution.

Lie on your back on a starry night and count the stars. Our cities have shut them out with ambient light and we forget to look up. Dark skies, however, hold testimony of the immensity of the heavens and the possibility of life beyond earth. The clay tablets of the Sumerians and legends of every people, speak of fire from the sky and giants and gods mating with humans.

The mysteries of the pyramids of Giza and the other pyramids of the Yucatan and Asia are examples of special places in the world built with astronomical exactitude.

Chaco Canyon…. the empires of the Incas… the mysteries of Angkor Watt. Chariots of the Gods! So many mysteries. So few answers.

Intelligent Design:

This is the newest hot term for those who fear religion. They swear this is a ploy by religionists to tempt our children with any thought other than evolution. I would simply ask what is there to fear?

Can't we all agree that life is very complex? I firmly believe we will never understand all the details. My study of the human body for the last 40 years finds me more humble every day. I personally cannot conceive of life spontaneously "evolving" from carbon, hydrogen and oxygen atoms.

It is hard to believe in no beginning and no end, because that is not in our experience. Everything we experience has a definite start and finish. But where did that carbon atom come from? No… ….. in the real beginning? Impossible question, huh?

I like believing that I have a divine nature. I like thinking I have a destiny. I like thinking that I am part of a magnificent plan of salvation and I am in preparation for the next chapter after this life. I like thinking that someone out there in another world or plane or space cares about me.

I like thinking there is order, not chaos, in my existence. I like my life and my concept of life! What is your honest belief in the nature of man?

I have spent years welcoming new spirits to this earth. I have seen the beat of a heart, like a flashing point of light in a 6 week embryo. I have seen a 12 week conception wave an arm and kick a leg. I have thrilled at the first gasp of air as the head squeezes into a new air filled world from a water-filled womb. I have witnessed the wonder and glory of life every day of my life.

As I wrote my thoughts in this book, I was once again reminded of how little we know and understand these bodies that are tabernacles to our souls. Is there a spark of the divine in each of us? What is your destiny? Is this really the only existence you have ever or will ever know?

For me it would be blasphemy to not acknowledge the hand of a greater being than I in creating the life I enjoy and witness all around. Andre Pare, a French surgeon in the Hundred Years War said, "I dress the wounds, but God heals them." With all the gadgetry of modern medicine, I still am not sure that we do much more than Andre Pare did to heal the wounds.

So what do you believe the origins of life to be?

The great thing is that you don't have to make a decision for anyone else but you. I would just ask you to remember sometime to drive out into the country and turn out the lights and look up at the sky. Breathtaking!

But even easier is to look into the eyes of a child or even into the mirror. You live with one of the greatest wonders of the universe.

I dare you to design a hand!

Lifetime Learning

I think most people will benefit by a re-evaluation of what they learned in school. It is unfortunate that our experience in school may determine our entire approach to learning the rest of our lives. You must be a lifetime student! The most dangerous position to be in in life is to think you know it all. Change is the most important factor in your life today. The answers are changing every day!

You can be a <u>MASTER</u> of change
or
a <u>VICTIM</u> of change.

Being able to learn is the key. Ninety percent
of what you now use in your job will change in
the next five years. The amount of knowledge
available to you will double every two to three
years! Seventy percent of Americans have not
bought a book in the last five years! You cannot
afford to "know it all."

Our schools were not designed to teach us to
learn. That's right. They were designed to train
us to be on time. They were designed to teach us
to not question authority. They were designed
to teach us to sit quietly for long periods of time.
They were designed to teach us a low level of
reading, writing and math. They were designed
to control creativity and original thought. They
were designed to teach us to sharpen our pencil
and ask permission to speak. They were designed
to teach us to follow directions and instructions.
They were designed to control the masses.
Schools have done a wonderful job of doing that.

The label we received those first months of school
will stay with us for life unless we realize the label

was artificial and only was a label applied to one way of learning.

Many of the problems of mass education are perpetuated by centuries old myths about learning and the brain. I have learned from the foremost educator of how we learn, Stephanie Burns, that we were educated to be forgetful about successes and to remember well our failures. She teaches learning strategies, which allow adults to retrain and relearn and shed the old labels.

You must understand that grades have nothing to do with your ability to succeed in life! There is in fact ……….

NO RELATIONSHIP BETWEEN GRADES IN SCHOOL AND SUCCESS IN LIFE!

So forget the past. Lets talk about your future. All people have brains with an extraordinary ability to learn. That is correct….ALL, not some.

If you can read this page, you have learned. If you can tie your shoes, you have learned. If you can drive a car, you have learned. If you can run a business, you have learned. If you can count to 100, you have learned. If you remember your keys, you have learned. If you can prepare a meal, you have learned. If you remember your friend's face, you have learned.

Why didn't school help you celebrate the right answers rather than accentuate the wrong answers. Did your teacher mark the wrong answers or the right answers? Why were there artificial levels to determine who got an A and who got an F? There were a few "A"s and a few "F"s, and then there was everyone else. Wasn't the grade more appropriately applied to the teacher who had failed and not the student?

YOU WERE BORN WITH EVERYTHING YOU NEED TO SUCCEED AS A LEARNER!

If you look at all you have learned you can't be stupid! The brain we had at birth is not the brain we have today. Only a small amount of brain development begins before birth. It is the world that develops the newborn brain. The world we live in changes our brains all the time. The number of brain cells cannot be changed, but how they communicate is directly related to how we use them.

If you cannot learn something it is often because you believe you cannot learn something. The problem is how you are trying to learn, not your inability to learn. Re-evaluate how you learn and change the method, don't accept a label.

One of the most dangerous thoughts is in regard to natural talent. Skills can almost always be developed. Those who become outstanding do it through discipline and practice. Often the only divergence between them and you is that they did it and you didn't. Don't fall into the trap of using the "talent" and "natural" labels as a reason to not even try. I don't believe anyone with a skill got that way without developing it through a lot of hard work. Decide what you want to do, and then do it.

Remember that learning is always an active process. You have to do something. Learning never happens in a passive way if it is meaningful. Everything you think you cannot learn is merely an activity that you have not approached with enough choices. We tend to go through life trying to learn the way we did in school. This is good if you made "A"s. If you made another grade, however, you need to change your approach to learning. You became an expert at getting "B"s. You need to change your learning style to get "A"s and you will get them. We teach students that there is only one way to learn. This was not true in the past and it is certainly not true today.

You may not remember anything you learned sitting in a desk at school, but you will never forget that Mary dropped her lunch tray on the floor and food went everywhere. What was the difference? If your teacher wrote a date on the blackboard you would struggle to remember it, but if she spray-painted it on the floor, you would never forget it. What was the difference? In the examples, they were so different that they were memorable. In fact they cannot be forgotten.

Our schools today should not prepare for jobs, but must prepare for life. Life is learning and every brain can do it. We survived the saber-toothed tiger with our brains not our brawn. You must learn how you learn and then be a lifetime learner.

Do not believe the lies you were taught in school. You are not too dumb. You are not too old. You are not too slow. You are not too poor. You are not too late.

We all have the rest of our lives to be, think, learn, and live whatever we want. Every year the *Forbes* magazine lists the 400 richest people in America. On that list, the high school dropouts are worth, on the average, 300 million more than the college graduates. They started earlier in life to succeed and did not fit in the system of education designed to control the masses and create employees.

The only question for you to ask is, "What do I want the rest of my life to be and how do I get it." HOW? That should be the only question you ask when considering any dream or goal. If you are human, you can do anything you think you can do, and I believe in you. Will you believe in yourself?

You must learn how you learn. We do not all learn the same way, but everyone can learn some way. I no longer believe in learning disabilities. We place the blame on learning failure on a mysterious neurological deficiency in the brain instead of the need to reform a system that just doesn't teach all children. We are sacrificing many of our children's minds to defend a system that does not work to protect the ego and jobs of education industry adults. Do not give up on your ability to learn or the ability of everyone of your children to learn.

There are at least seven styles of learning, and school only uses one. Let us look at a few of the most common styles not addressed by our traditional school system.

1. You learn best by experience. People who learn this way are always asking the question, "WHY?" or " WHY NOT?" What you are looking for is some personal meaning or relevance for the information and skills you are learning. This is the learner who gets suppressed by a school system that answers questions by saying 'Because, I told you to."

2. You learn by gathering facts and data and then thinking about them. You are always looking for the answer to the question, "WHAT?" You are hungry for data to feed to your brain. You have little need for experience. The data you receive creates new information as you link it to data you have already stored. You are an observer. You learn by watching not doing. Schools were designed for this type of learner.

3. You like to learn by figuring out what makes things work. You want to know what makes

them useful. You want answers to the question, "HOW?" Information and skills need to be practical for you. You usually find that school misses the point. You are an experimenter and want to take things apart.

4. You learn by experience and experimenting. You find the classroom intolerable. You are the learner that school destroys. You create whole new ways of doing and thinking. The question you need to have answered is, "WHAT IF?" You will do almost anything but what is asked of you. This type of learner frequently is put on drugs, expelled from school, drops out and runs away from home, or is labeled as having a learning disability.

Most of us use each of these types in our approach to learning. The most successful use all of them selectively when they are most appropriate. Each of us has a predominant learning style, however, and that limits our ability to learn in an inflexible system like organized schools. We all didn't learn to walk on the same day of life. Why do we insist that we do multiplication tables on the same day of life?

All I ask is that you realize that whoever you are, you can learn whatever you want. To believe less than that is an injustice to the marvelous brain you were born with. Do not accept labels. Do not accept the lies you were taught in school. Decide what you want, and then get what you want. Commit today to be a lifetime student. Believe you can self educate yourself, because I know you can.

Two of the people I acknowledge in the beginning of this book, Mark Hughes and Joseph Smith, Jr., did not complete even a high school education. They were not products of organized school education. They would have probably been lousy factory workers, yet they both influenced millions of lives. They are among the most noteworthy people in my life. Their wisdom was not limited by what people said or the world's opinion of them. They were brave enough to do what they felt was right. They did not let governments or public opinion steal their dreams or change their missions. They did whatever it took to believe in their cause and learned the skills that they needed. They were lifetime learners.

Napoleon Hill said, "Anything the human mind can conceive and believe, it can achieve." I know that is true. So what do you want? Feed your brain and exercise your brain, and you can be and do whatever you want. You were born to succeed.

Your DNA was programmed to succeed and survive. No matter what you believed in the past, believe now that you can and must learn. Your life depends on it.

Children:
Food For
Thought

Where do we start? Everyone in the world worries about his or her children. They are the future. We share our DNA with them and want their life to be better than ours. This is a universal desire of human beings. It has not changed for 50,000 years.

So what do we need to know about life to insure our children will have a better life? Does that mean more money? Does that mean more material things? Does that mean better health? Does that mean more happiness? Does that mean more years of life?

In reality, if you do not have your health, you have a major challenge in life. Health will affect our child's ability to prepare for adulthood.

There are several child epidemics growing in the world.

Autism
Attention Deficit Hyperactivity Defect
Behavior Problems
Learning Disabilities
Obesity
Type II Diabetes
Fatigue
Suicide
Teen Pregnancy

Mostly mental, but also physical problems occur at alarming rates in our offspring. There have been many opinions as to why these exist. I would again admonish you to remember that 90% of all we hear is opinion. Lets look back in time to when these were not epidemic diseases. We don't have to go back far. These are actually problems that have risen in the last hundred years. Perhaps only three generations have seen these changes occur.

So what has changed?

Life
Technology
Medicine
Schools
Families
Physical Activity
Food

Lets take each one individually.

Life

Where do we start here? One hundred years ago
life was similar to three hundred years ago. We
traveled by foot, boat or horse. We played simple
games depending on our imagination or with
simple toys like marbles, dolls, balls, and hoops.
We did not travel long distances unless migrating
to a new home. We oriented our lives to the
seasons, daylight and our families. Books were
treasures and limited. Education was a privilege,
not a right. Life and death were religious
experiences.

Technology

Television has been a major influence on the
youth for 50 years. It has become the primary
educator of our children. That's right. Television
educates every minute it is watched. Even
when turned on as background noise, television
is inputting ideas and information into our
children's minds. This passive education sells
products, food, ideas and values. To not accept
this is naive.

Computers and the Internet make information

instantaneous today. Anything and everything can be found online. Only your imagination will limit what you can find there 24 hours a day.

Video games often teach violence and disregard for life and society. They can be as addicting as drugs, as they stimulate the pleasure centers of our children's brains.

Music is available as never before. No longer is it the harmonica, guitar or banjo around the hearth of our home. The special experiences of hearing the town band concert on Sunday afternoon or the piano in the local church or school are no longer an events to be excited about today. Within minutes, you can download any song into your MP3 player and in a device the size of a box of matches, you can store 20 hours of continuous songs. This would be truly unbelievable even 10 years ago. The lyrics of these songs also teach, even if only heard as background noise. Remember how easy it was to learn the lyrics of a song in school rather than the cold hard facts in science class?

And what about videotapes and DVDs? Remember, a picture is worth a thousand words. Once again, more input into our children's brains.

Then there are the automobile and airplanes and motorcycles and space shuttles and cruise ships and theme parks! Where will it end?

Medicine

We have changed from a society that used doctors as a last resort, to a society totally dependent on the prescription and over the counter drugs of the world. We want perfect health at any cost. Over the last 100 years we have moved from prevention of disease to an emphasis on treatment of disease. Now as our children share the diseases once thought to be exclusive to adults, we question the last 100 years, and that is why you are reading this book.

Now is the time for us to take back our health and the personal responsibility for it. We can affect our children's health. The good news is that it is not ever too late to make positive changes. Let's use our doctors as an educational source rather than as drug dealers or prescription machines.

I was told the first day of medical school that I would only help one out of every three patients I saw each day. In fact, it was very sobering when

I was told that I would actually make one out of three worse as a result of my treatment. The remaining one out of three would get better or worse regardless of what I did.

Probably the most significant thing that medicine has done to lengthen life and relieve pain and suffering was the discovery of antibiotics. Infection was the major killer along with accidents and trauma throughout mankind's history. This discovery happened only 60 years ago! Yes, we do all kinds of surgery with modern anesthetic methods, but without antibiotics we would die from the surgery.

So with our children it is the prevention, not the treatment, that must become a passion. Trauma and accidents are still one of the major dangers of youth, as we try new things and have a disregard for the risks of new adventures.

Immunizations have played a major role in eliminating the epidemics of the past. However, much of medicine is focused on treating symptoms of disease and not looking to the core cause of the symptoms. Many questions still remain to be answered about the real effects of even immunizations on our immune system.

Schools

This subject is covered in detail in the chapter on lifetime learning, but it is a key to our children's mental health. Our schools still function on a basic level like the schools of 100 years ago. They teach us to be on time. They teach us to conform. They discourage creativity. They label us for life. They reinforce the lies we live by. They limit our ability to succeed. They produce perfect factory workers with minimal skills who will follow direction without question. It has nothing to do with education. It is about training for a life of quiet desperation and unfulfilled potential. Read the chapter "Lifetime of Learning."

Families

The definition has certainly changed and is different with every society and culture in the world. Within America the definitions are multiple. For many children their family is a gang. The traditional family creates children, provides for them physically and emotionally until they reach maturity, and then they leave to create their own families.

We need to be loved. We need to feel someone cares about us. We need to feel safe. The dysfunction of adults is passed on to their children. Whether it is a "good" or "bad" family is in the eye of the beholder. But this I know. Everyone should feel safe and loved. Without that, there cannot be health.

Physical Activity

Physical activity is certainly different today than 100 years ago. We often labored as children on the farm or in a factory. We actually didn't walk great distances daily, because we didn't go very far from our homes as a rule. As children in middle class families we actually did about the same as many children today, especially if involved with a sports team. Girls on the other hand had less physical activity as they learned to sew, cook and keep house. Beating carpets, washing clothes and hauling water were physical, however.

If we go all the way back to our roots, there is an entirely different story when we consider physical activity. Children were not let out of the village walls or the cave. It was too dangerous. They spent time playing simple and usually quiet games: drawing in the dirt, collecting bugs, telling stories, listening to stories, being groomed by their elders, carrying a younger sibling, helping with the chores around the house, waiting for the hunting party to come home, waiting for the time we could join them and get some excitement in our lives, helping the women of the tribe to gather what nature grew close to our homes. These activities were not much different than sitting in front of a computer or watching TV or coloring in a book.

Today we do not allow our children to play spontaneously in our yards or parks for fear of molestation from mentally sick adults. I grew up wandering all over my neighborhood, riding the bus and riding my bike pretty much at will. I just needed to tell my parents approximately where I was going and when I would be home. Not so today. A bus or carpool picks us up at our doors and returns us there. We only leave to do organized activities that are deemed safe by our parents.

We need to teach our children to be safe and have "street smarts" so they are not lured by the depraved of our society. Once again we see adults as the source of most children's problems.

My recommendation is to teach our children to stretch, and walk and jump and swing and have fun with movement. Dance is probably the perfect blend of aesthetic and athletic. It is good for the mind as well as the body. Safe touching is good.

What about jump rope and hopscotch? All movement is good. We want to teach lifetime movement that will keep our bodies flexible and supple.

What about competitive activities for our children? Here comes my opinion again. How many children have permanently injured their joints for the team and been unable to pursue recreation the rest of their lives because of competitive athletics?

Usually the adults are the ones who introduce the need for competition. If left to their own, kids just like to play. I am of the era when we would meet at the local park after school, choose up sides and play flag football or softball without any adult supervision. Everyday new teams were created and often we didn't even keep score. No one cared who won? There was always tomorrow! If we had fun, we all won! Why did we let adults ruin the fun of the games and turn them into wars?

Today even our vocabulary is filled with sports examples, which further emphasize competition, not recreation. My plea is to let our kids have fun while they can. Life is competitive enough as it is. Let's let children be children! You should not have to win to have fun. When you play, you should always win!

Food

Food does not equal nutrition today for our children. Food equals drugs! I have left my passion for last, because I think it is the most important ingredient to health for our children. All the topics have their place. Balance, however, is an important concept.

My opinion is that almost everything we feed our children in America is unfit for child consumption! That is a pretty broad statement, but I hope to convince you I am on the right track. Please read on.

Remember our DNA was created to keep us alive, thin, and healthy with the food available in nature. Today we do not feed our children anything derived from nature. NOTHING!!!!! Get the picture? You name me one naturally occurring food your children eat.

I'm waiting.............
If you said walnuts or pine nuts, you were right.
Nuts and perhaps wild berries are about it.
Maybe some dried fruit!

EVERYTHING ELSE IS MAN MADE!!!!!!!

We have spent tens of thousands of years making our natural food artificial. We have continually tried to add herbs, spices, and chemicals to make our natural food not nutrition, but recreation and a feel-good experience. Primitive man rarely said "This tastes good." He was just looking for food to keep him and his family alive for one more day. They ate to live. We live to eat. That is the fundamental problem.

We give our kids what they want to eat, not what they need to eat. It is not lack of exercise making them fat and sick.....

IT IS LACK OF NUTRITION !!!!!!!!

Doesn't that make sense? Isn't it logical? Can you find a good argument for what I am saying?

No. This is as close to fact as I can get. My opinion? Yes! True? You decide. This I know. What we are doing is killing our kids! How much longer do we do the same thing and expect a different result? We must realize what we have done to undermine their health. It is not too late to take responsibility and make a change. Remember: be a master of change, not a victim of change.

This is not good news for humans who use food to reward themselves and give meaning to their stress-filled lives. Many people feel that life is not worth living without wonderful tasting food. I understand. I admit to being addicted to our modern food. I just must warn you that we are trading pleasure for life. Is this what we want for our children?

All of our children need fish oil supplements of pharmaceutical grade to build their brains. Not some, ALL! The facts are not debatable. Our children's brains grow for two years after they are born. They are made of fat. We then replace those cells every day for the rest of our lives...... forever. Read the chapter on Omega Fats to get the whole story, but our kid's brains must be fed fat in order to function properly.

Then there is the grain factor. I have been told all of my life that whole grain was good. "Wheat for man", was a mantra around our house as my mom ground her wheat and made the bread that stayed with you for two days after you ate it. The United States Government still places grain as the widest path in their food pyramid. So what is the truth? Read the chapter "Going Against the Grain."

Our kids need eggs, meat, fruit, NOT grain for breakfast. That is what their DNA was intended to be fed. Protein shakes are one of the good artificial foods that will get them started right with a little added omega 3 fat to jumpstart their brains for the day.

Sugar is also not good, but I think the grain is actually the most detrimental to their health. Today, unfortunately, fifty percent of children's calories or more come from grain that we were never intended to eat at all. If you want to kill your kid give him grain.

This lack of nutrition is compounded by the drug – chemical dependence we have produced in our children from the first year of life. They never get hungry, they just have the drug levels drop and need another fix to keep them from withdrawing.

Ask yourself, why do they call it a "Happy Meal?" Why do we hear children mimic their parents saying they would "kill" for their favorite fast food? They want drugs just the same as the heroin addict. Can you understand what is going on? You are slaves to the food sellers of America, even if you live in a foreign country today. We are exporting drugs and malnutrition around the world disguised as "Happy Meals." We are no better than the Colombian Drug Cartels!

I have learned as a State Senator to follow the dollar. Profit is the name of the game. What was perhaps ignorance and naïve experimentation for better tasting food one thousand years ago, has been taken to a criminal level in the quest for more money and hence more power. We are a hedonistic society bent on self-destruction and we have shared that with our precious next generation.

Even our schools perpetuate the health crisis with the school lunches approved by the dietician for the school system. Ever notice how many dietitians are over weight? We finance school activities selling drugs to our kids out of vending machines.

THAT IS EXACTLY WHAT WE ARE DOING!

ADD, ADHD, learning disabilities, depression, suicide, behavior disorders, anger, violence, chronic illness, diabetes, allergies, asthma and obesity have all been linked to our artificial food. Put a kid in front of a TV or computer or even at a school desk and feed him unnatural, disease producing food and you have today's youth and the challenges of health. To make things worse, the TV sells him the drugs with a clown named Ronald!

I challenge you to think about what I have said. Even a small change in the right direction will make a difference in your child's health. What I say is logical. Unfortunately, you, like everyone else, just don't want to hear it. So your fall-back position will be more visits to the doctor, more prescription medications and more rationalization in order to support you and your family's drug habit.

A little severe you say? This chapter is written as much to my family and me, as it is to each of you. Our children's brains are the future of mankind. Without them we are doomed. With them we can continue to survive and to thrive. We are the descendants of our ancestor's brains and their ability to survive, in spite of overwhelming adversities and challenges.

Why We Die.........

The five leading causes of death in America today are:

1. <u>Heart Disease:</u> 1.5 million deaths per year. Heart attack every 20 seconds in America.

2. Cancer: 600,000 die per year.

3. Modern Healthcare: Prescription Drugs, Physician Errors, and Hospitals account for over 250,000 deaths a year in America.

4. Hypertension and Stroke: deaths and debilitation.

5. Diabetes: epidemic with 16 million in the US and accounting for over 140,000 deaths per year.

Many deaths in America are diet related. Therefore, nutrition should be good medicine.

Causes 1,2,4 and 5 are dealt with throughout this book and will not be covered here.

Because of the shock value, lets just get the facts out of the way about cause number three: Modern Healthcare. All of these statistics come from the Journal of the American Medical Association (JAMA July 26,2000; 284 (4):483-5) as a result of the Institute of Medicine Report December 1999.

Doctors Are
The Third Leading Cause
of Death in the US,
Causing 250,000 Deaths
Every Year!

The author is Dr. Barbara Starfield of the Johns Hopkins School of Hygiene and Public Health, and she describes how the US health care system may contribute to poor health.

ALL THESE ARE DEATHS PER YEAR:

- **12,000 -- unnecessary surgery**

- **7,000 -- medication errors in hospitals**

- **20,000 -- other errors in hospitals**

- **80,000 -- infections in hospitals**

- **106,000 -- non-error, negative effects of drugs**

These total 250,000 deaths per year from iatrogenic causes!!

What does the word iatrogenic mean?

Induced in a patient by a physician's activity, manner, or therapy. Used especially in relation to a complication of treatment.

Dr. Starfield offers several warnings in interpreting these numbers:

- First, most of the data are derived from studies in hospitalized patients.

- Second, these estimates are for deaths only and do not include negative effects that are associated with disability or discomfort.

- Third, the estimates of death due to error are lower than those in the Institute of Medicine report.

If the higher estimates are used, the deaths due to iatrogenic causes would range from 230,000 to 284,000. In any case, 225,000 deaths per year constitute, the third leading cause of death in the United States, after deaths from heart disease and cancer. Even if these figures are overestimated, there is a wide margin between these numbers of deaths and the next leading cause of death (cerebrovascular disease or stroke).

Another analysis concluded that between 4% and 18% of patients experience negative effects in outpatient settings due to:

- 116 million extra physician visits

- 77 million extra prescriptions

- 17 million emergency department visits

- 8 million hospitalizations

- 3 million long-term admissions

- 199,000 additional deaths

- $77 billion in extra costs

The high cost of the health care system is considered to be a deficit, but seems to be tolerated under the assumption that better health results from more expensive care.

However, evidence from a few studies indicates that as many as 20% to 30% of all patients receive inappropriate care.

An estimated 44,000 to 98,000 among them die each year as a result of medical errors.

This might be tolerated if it resulted in better health, but does it? Of 13 countries in a recent comparison, the United States ranks an average of 12th (second from the bottom) for 16 available health indicators. More specifically, the ranking of the US on several indicators was:

- 13th (last) for low-birth-weight percentages

- 13th for neonatal mortality and infant mortality overall 14th

- 11th for post neonatal mortality

- 13th for years of potential life lost (excluding external causes)

- 11th for life expectancy at 1 year for females, 12th for males

- 10th for life expectancy at 15 years for females, 12th for males

- 10th for life expectancy at 40 years for females, 9th for males

- 7th for life expectancy at 65 years for females, 7th for males

- 3rd for life expectancy at 80 years for females, 3rd for males

- 10th for age-adjusted mortality

The poor performance of the US was recently confirmed by a World Health Organization study, which used different data and ranked the United States as 15th among 25 industrialized countries.

There is a perception that the American public "behaves badly" by smoking, drinking, and perpetrating violence." However the data does not support this assertion.

- The proportion of females who smoke ranges from 14% in Japan to 41% in Denmark; in the United States, it is 24% (fifth best). For males, the range is from 26% in Sweden to 61% in Japan; it is 28% in the United States (third best).

- The US ranks fifth best for alcoholic

beverage consumption.

- The US has relatively low consumption of animal fats (fifth lowest in men aged 55-64 years in 20 industrialized countries) and the third lowest mean cholesterol concentrations among men aged 50 to 70 years among 13 industrialized countries.

These estimates of death due to error are lower than those in a recent Institutes of Medicine report, and if the higher estimates are used, the deaths due to iatrogenic causes would range from 230,000 to 284,000.

Even at the lower estimate of 225,000 deaths per year, this constitutes the third leading cause of death in the US, following heart disease and cancer.

Lack of technology is certainly not a contributing factor to the US's low ranking.

- Among 29 countries, the United States is second only to Japan in the availability of magnetic resonance imaging units and computed tomography scanners per million population.

- Japan, however, ranks highest on health, whereas the US ranks among the lowest.

- It is possible that the high use of technology

in Japan is limited to diagnostic technology not matched by high rates of treatment, whereas in the US, high use of diagnostic technology may be linked to more treatment.

Supporting this possibility are data showing that the number of employees per bed in the United States hospitals is highest among the countries ranked, whereas they are very low in Japan. Hospital employees are even far lower in Japan than can be accounted for by the common practice of having family members, rather than hospital staff, provide the amenities of hospital care.

As a State Senator, who deals daily with the deficits in the budget caused by the exploding cost of healthcare, I am sobered as I realize we do not really get better results no matter how much money we put into the US Healthcare System. No other country in the world spends even half as much per person for healthcare as we do in America. More dollars to do more of the same is not the answer.

Obesity: The Shape of Health Today......

Obesity now kills 300,000 Americans per year and health-care costs associated with obesity top $100 billion annually.

The World Bank has estimated that 12 percent of the U.S. national health-care budget is spent treating obesity. It is also estimated that treatment of obesity related illnesses costs another 40%.

The Cost of Obesity:

April 4, 2002: 4:20 PM EST
Leslie Haggin Geary, CNN/Money
Staff Writer

> "NEW YORK (CNN/Money) - Dieters may want to lose weight to look more attractive. But experts say there's another reason to shed pounds: Obesity costs money -- a lot of it."

There are other costs as well. One study found that businesses lose $47.6 billion annually due to the indirect costs of obesity, such as lost productivity and higher absenteeism among excessively overweight workers, not to mention the higher rate of injuries among the obese and workman's comp. claims.

Obesity is defined by federal guidelines using the body-mass index (BMI). A BMI score of 30 or more is classified as obese and 25-29.9 is overweight.

I personally do not think this is a good measure of real optimal weight. It works for people in the average range, but has no validity for the extremes. A weight lifter will not have a correct score on a BMI, which only takes into account the height and weight of an individual. The standard BMI categories do not differentiate between male and female adults and do not factor for such variables as body frames. Many people are misclassified, and I feel we should abandon using these tables

In my own practice we use ElectroLipoGraphy (ELG) from BioAnalogics. I would encourage you to go to appendix VI for a complete discussion of body composition evaluation.

Today, six out of 10 American adults -- some 120 million --are overweight or obese, according to the National Institutes of Health. Roughly 24 percent of adults are obese -- more than double the amount a decade ago. One in five children qualify as obese.

Despite America's obsession with weight and the popularity of fad diets, the sheer cost of obesity, and its epidemic sweep over the country, has gone largely unnoticed and untreated by doctors as well as politicians. This is despite the fact that, obesity now causes more health problems than smoking, heavy drinking, or poverty.

Obese individuals spend 36 percent more on health care, and 21 percent more on medication, than daily smokers and heavy drinkers. Smoking used to be the big deal in the 1960s, and obesity levels stayed level back then. Weight has just exploded in the last 15 years.

The IRS now recognizes obesity as a disease and as long as a diet program is prescribed by a doctor, it can qualify for a tax deduction. Previously, weight-loss expenses have not qualified for a deduction if a person's weight did not contribute to other illnesses such as hypertension, diabetes or heart disease. The new rule recognizes that obesity is a disease in its own right, thus making it easier for individuals to write off their out-of-pocket expenses. The ruling should help a considerable number of people. The cost of special diet foods can't be included, since individuals have to pay for their food whether they're losing weight or not. Medical costs can be deducted only if they exceed 7.5 percent of a person's adjusted gross income. This strict requirement keeps most Americans from claiming medical deductions in general. According to the IRS, only 4 percent of filers deduct their medical costs. For more information about various medical costs that may qualify for a deduction see IRS Publication 502.

It is far from clear whether insurance companies will begin to cover weight-loss treatments. Good science about the effectiveness of particular treatments and long term success will need to be demonstrated before they become benefits on most policies.

My bias is still that obesity is caused by our unnatural diets that consist of artificial, feel good food. We have adequate calories but we are malnourished. We send messages to our body that our food supply is precarious and in self defense the body stores fat to keep us alive.

Only through perfect nutrition will we achieve our optimal weight and maintain it for life. Nutrition, not starvation, is the only answer.

I actually cannot understand how with the basic rule of physicians to first do no harm, that we still can justify permanent malnutrition, malabsorption, through gastric bypass surgery in all its forms. This cannot be without lifelong harm. Why does organized medicine not only endorse, but actually encourage such a dangerous means to get to an unhealthy result? The world has gone crazy in its attempt to get to an end result. Isn't anyone questioning and thinking about what is being done?

Traditional Approach to Weight Loss

"Eat Less"
"Exercise More"

No studies have been done to prove this works to permanently allow you to maintain your optimal weight. Doesn't everyone know that is true? Calories in and calories out……. Yes, starvation makes you lose, but once you eat your body is storing fat in a survival mode. This is another "Urban Legend!" If it worked, America would be thin!

Total Cellular Nutrition

Protein
Carbohydrates
Fats and Oils
Vitamins

Minerals
Micronutrients
Water

All day, everyday, for a lifetime.

We must eat to be healthy, and if we take in the right nutrition we will automatically be our right weight. There are no fat wild animals!!!!!! If you've seen one jack rabbit you have seen them all. Wild animals eat what nature provides. Wild animals in zoos, however, have the same diseases our pets have. Wild animals in nature almost never have these.

Because of how long we will live, nutrition is even more important today. Cellular Nutrition is about believing you can make a difference in your health and taking control of your life. Only through eating will you maintain your optimal weight and lose fat while building muscle.

When you starve or diet do you lose fat or muscle? You lose muscle. Wouldn't you rather eat than starve? Your body would rather be fed. What kind of a message do you send daily to your metabolism by even skipping meals?

What happens to your body when you starve?

1. Your metabolism slows down.

2. Calories are saved.

3. Muscle is burned for energy.

4. Any food eaten is stored as fat if possible to prepare for a prolonged period of decreased nutrition.

5. When the diet is over, fat is replaced and more stored to prepare for the next famine.

6. Add exercise to starvation and you stress the body even more by increasing the caloric requirements without giving nutrition. Hence more muscle is sacrificed.

More fat and less muscle is not the answer. Your resting metabolism is 14 times your lean body mass. Less muscle lowers your lean body mass, your metabolism and encourages weight gain.

Cellular nutrition, not starvation is the key to weight loss success. Only through adequate cellular nutrition can exercise be safe and

effective in building muscle and breaking down fat. Dieters have less muscle, more fat, and lower metabolisms than people who have always eaten.

Your goal should be as much lean muscle and as little stored fat as possible. This, however, will be a bad tactic if we have a real famine.

You will die early (which may also be a blessing).

If there isn't a famine, however, you will have less cancer, heart disease, hypertension, stroke and diabetes.

Dr. Komadina Nutrition Pearls

Dr. David Heber from UCLA taught me how to design a perfect proportion of nutrition components in a diet. It is interesting when we talk about diet in humans we assume starvation. Diet for our pets means good nutrition.

We call protein, fats and carbohydrates macronutrients because they are big.

The goal is one gram of protein for each pound of lean body mass.

The average American Female needs :
   85-110 grams of protein / day and 1200-1500 calories / day

 The Average American Male:
   120-175 grams of protein / day and 1800-3,000 calories / day

The Basal Metabolic Rate in calories is 14 times the pounds of Lean Body Mass. This is the calories burned at rest. Subtract 500 calories or increase the burning of 500 calories with exercise to lose weight.

29% of calories from protein
51% of calories from colorful vegetables and fruits
20% of calories from good fats

One serving of fruits and vegetables a day from the seven different color groups.

Dr. Heber also advocates avoiding what he calls "trigger" foods, such as nuts, cheese, pizza, salad dressings, butter, margarine, mayonnaise, red meat, fatty fish, frozen yogurt, ice cream, cookies, pastries, and cakes. He believes that these foods "turn you on and make you fat." His advice is to avoid these foods forever, including the low-fat or fat-free versions. He believes that by avoiding these foods one can learn to lose the desire for them. He also believes that no one can learn to eat smaller portions of his or her favorite foods.

I know you can lose your unwanted and unneeded fat. We must have some fat, but there is an optimal amount for health. The BioAnalogics ELG machine will give you the best indication of your healthy weight range. For most women it is between 18 and 28% body fat and for men 8-18%. I attribute the difference to the fact that biologically the female of the species is worth more and needs more "life insurance" in case there is a famine. My female patients tell me the difference is that men do not have brains (remember brains are 80% fat.)!

The Gastrointestinal Tract: Through, Not In, The Body

Our body has two barriers to toxins from the outside world. The skin protects us from the outside entrance of toxins. What most people don't realize is that, from your mouth to your rectum, the intestinal tract, is also "outside" your body in reality. Food we eat is just "passing through" a tunnel of outside skin type cells that very selectively let foreign substances into our actual bodies. If this were not true, what goes in our mouths would literally kill us.

Let's take a look at the journey our food takes.

Our Mouth:

Here are found very special cells that can tolerate very wide ranges of temperature, and forms of food. The teeth exist merely to make the solid food smaller, as we begin to liquefy everything that begins the journey through our body. Taste buds help us reject very toxic substances immediately.

Our Esophagus:

The tube that carries the chopped up, cooled or warmed food from our mouth to the stomach is called the esophagus. It is the laundry chute that quickly moves things down. It is not meant to hold food for any length of time. Food caught here tends to come back up. Transport down is its only job.

Our Stomach:

Here is where the powerful acids mix with the chopped food and liquefy it for further transport and absorption. The cells that line our stomach were designed to secrete and withstand this acid. If the valve between the stomach and the esophagus is weak, the acid refluxes (moves back up) into the esophagus and burns this delicate organ giving "Gastro-Esophageal Reflux Disease" (GERD) or what we used to call heartburn.

Our Small Intestine:

Twenty-two feet of small intestine represents the workhorse of digestion and absorption. The "skin" here has been modified to continue the breakdown of the food into its smallest nutrition units: simple sugars, amino acids and individual fatty acid molecules. Its job is to keep everything else OUT of our body. Anything else might kill us. Remember you eat bacteria, toxins and yes, even manure, every day on the food placed in your mouth. The lining of the 22 feet of small bowel is humped up into "villi" to increase the surface area for more efficient absorption and digestion. These villi are further covered by micro-villi or what is referred to as a "brush border," making the surface area even greater. Amazing as it may seem (and everything about our bodies is amazing) these folds (villi) and their

brush boarder give a huge working surface area. Less than one half inch (1 cm) of small bowel lining if smoothed out, would cover a doubles tennis court!

After the digestive enzymes chop proteins into individual amino acids and carbohydrates into simple sugars, they are admitted into our blood stream through very tight joints between the cells, that keep everything else out. Individual fatty acids are first admitted to the cells of the brush border, converted into triglycerides, and then sent via the lymphatic system to the blood and on to the liver for processing. This is what happens in a normal small intestine. All other substances are kept out.

The key to health lies in this system functioning correctly. Any disruption can affect our health and our life. The key is that the "Tight Joints" between the small bowel's cells, only let through water, simple nutrients, and minerals. These tight joints screen out larger molecules of partially digested food, fiber, bacteria, parasites, chemicals and toxins mixed with our food. Sounds simple. Sounds perfect. It is both, when it works as designed.

Our Large Intestine or Colon:

Unlike the small bowel, which gets rid of bacteria if at all possible, the large bowel lives in harmony with friendly bacteria. These break down fiber, creating a fatty acid by-product called butyric acid, that nourishes the lining of the colon. The colon can then carry out its main job of absorbing water out of the nutritional waste dumped into it by the small bowel and forming a package of waste we call a "bowel movement." This again is a perfect system when functioning as designed.

Our Rectum or Anus:

The last part of the tunnel, passing through but not in our body, is the rectum and its valve called the anal sphincter. They hold in the raw sewage from what went in our mouth, until it can be conveniently deposited out of the body.

I hope this gives you an understanding of the pathway taken by the food you eat each day. Now let's talk about what can go wrong and the huge part artificial nutrition and unnatural food like grain and also beans (legumes) play in the cycle of human disease and health.

Going Against The Grain...

It is difficult for me to write about the risks of eating grain when I was raised to view grain, and especially wheat, as a gift given humans to allow them to eat nutritious and cheap food. My forefathers walked across the plains to the West in the 1800s. They survived the trip sometimes eating only wheat that had been planted by the pioneers who went before them, expressly for the feeding of those who followed. Was it possible that this grain was a gift to prevent death in times of famine and need, but not for daily consumption? That was a very conflicting thought in my mind. Doesn't everyone know that whole grains are good? I mean, look at the U.S. Government food pyramid!

COULD THE GOVERNMENT BE WRONG?

Here is much food, if not grain, for thought. You must make your own decision. I will still store grain for the possible famine or social or natural disaster. Grain will allow my family to survive. The question is what to do when there are times of plenty and any type of food is available?

No human ate grain during the Ice Age or before. We probable tried to chew it as we watched the animals eat it, but it was unfit for human consumption. We didn't have the multi-chambered stomachs to digest the tough protective coat of the raw grain. We didn't throw up our food and chew it again like the camels and cows. We didn't eat our bowel movements like the rabbit. We were not naturally intended to eat grain, otherwise we would have been born with the anatomy and physiology to digest it. Today it makes up 75% of the calories eaten by Americans. Those calories are also almost totally genetically engineered grains.

About 10 thousand years ago, that all changed. The people of the Middle East discovered by drying, grinding, and cooking grain it could be eaten and some life sustaining nutrition derived from it. They artificially did what the multi-chambered stomach of the bison, deer, elephant, and mammoth had done naturally.

The next step was to plant and grow the seeds, and agriculture was born. Grains were continually changed over the centuries to the point that what we eat today could not reseed itself and grow without man's help. The grain we eat today is totally man made. It is artificial food. Corn today, for instance, has fish DNA to make it more drought and insect resistant. Some one must ask, if the bugs won't eat it, should you and I? Interesting question, huh?

Our brains had helped us create a reliable food source. Because we were able to eat the newly processed grain, does not mean we were designed or meant to eat it. It was a survival food, which could keep us alive in times of famine and which could be stored, in the unprocessed state, for years. It allowed great cities to be built and civilizations to develop with all its blessings and its curses. It allowed our forefathers to migrate across America, and around the world, with an easily carried food supply. Grain also had the side effect of making us feel full, happy and gave a sense of well-being.

Scurvy and Beri-Beri were testament, however, that it was not the "Staff of Life." Grain was a <u>survival food</u> and incomplete nutrition for the human body. Wheat, while keeping us alive, also caused autoimmune disease and rheumatoid arthritis in some of our ancestors and our families today. Archeologist never find signs of arthritis in the bones of ancient hunter-gatherers they unearth. Arthritis is very common in the bones of ancient agricultural people.

It was not a food naturally created for human consumption. Most of us tolerate grains to a point, but they pose a definite health risk to all. Eating grain isn't overtly poisoning most of us with obvious disease, but it is causing many hidden problems. These health problems range from the autoimmune diseases of rheumatoid arthritis, lupus and multiple sclerosis, to inflammatory bowel disease and celiac sprue. Even mental illness including Alzheimer's disease is linked to the consumption of grain. As Michael Eades, M.D. states, "We created huge problems for our bodies when we hammered our spears into plowshares."

Now lets look at what can go wrong and the huge part grain and also beans (legumes) play in the cycle of disease and health caused by dysfunction of our gastrointestinal tract and immune system. This is how the system is disrupted by consuming foods we were never designed to eat: most specifically grain and beans.

Leaky Gut Syndrome

In the chapter on how the gastrointestinal tract processed food, there was a discussion of the importance of the "tight junctions" between the cells of the small bowel and how they kept large molecules, toxins and bacteria from entering the body and blood stream. When these tight junctions become loose, the system breaks down, and we are in danger of being killed by those foreign substances. Let's look at how that happens in people eating a typical Western Diet today.

Remember the tight joints effectively let into the blood stream only simple sugars from carbohydrates, water and individual amino acids from protein. The simple fatty acids from fat eaten go into the lymph of the brush boarder of the villi. The tight junctions should keep out bacteria, parasites, incompletely digested

starches, fiber, proteins and fats as well as chemicals and toxins in our food. These are left in the intestine and passed into the colon by the rhythmic contractions of the muscles in the wall of the bowel. They then become our bowel movements. This rhythm is called peristalsis. When these tight joints leak, huge problems occur in this perfectly balanced system designed for the food eaten by our ancestors, tens of thousands of years ago.

Lets talk about bacteria and parasites first. To do us harm they must attach to the wall of our GI tract. In the stomach there is a thick mucus gel that coats the surface and prevents attachment. In the small intestine no such mucous exists. Remember, the small bowel is made for absorption. The tight junctions won't let the bacteria in, and the waves of peristalsis keep the bacteria moving so it does not have time to attach to the walls. Also the surface cells of the small bowel are continuously sloughing off and carrying away any recently attached bacteria or parasite. This sloughing and renewal of the surface of the small bowel actually completely replaces the lining cells every four to five days.

If a bacteria or parasite does become attached, the immune system kills it in a healthy gut. In a healthy gut this system effectively eliminates any unwanted invasion of microbes. Today, because of our artificial diets, it has been estimated that two-thirds of our entire immune defense activity in the body is taking place on the surface of our gastrointestinal tract! Can you now see how what you eat can affect your entire ability to fight off infections and your overall health?

Our Small Bowel Is A War Zone!!!

There are some very hostile infections. Cholera, amoebic dysentery, typhoid, and various viruses can overwhelm the system by sheer numbers or poisons (toxins) they produce. There can also be mechanical problems like slowing of the movement of the bowel following abdominal surgery. This slowing can allow the infection bacteria to attach and damage the tight joints through swelling and inflammation.

The most common problem, however, is not an exotic infection or a surgery. The most common problems arise out of the consumption of grains and beans. There are actually natural anti-nutrients in grain that discouraged our primitive ancestors from eating the seed. The plant needed the seed to survive, to propagate the plant season to season. Today even processing the grain and legumes (beans) doesn't eliminate the anti-nutrients that damage the human intestine.

The Western Diet, rich in grain and sugars, overwhelms the ability of the gut to digest and absorb simple food units. Partially digested sugars and starches are sent into the colon where there are many bacteria not present in the small bowel. When loads of incompletely digested grain and beans enter the colon there is a veritable feeding frenzy, with resulting fermentation creating alcohols and gasses. Pressure builds up in the colon from the process, causing the fermenting waste to flush backwards reentering the small intestine. This toxic mass of bacteria and fermenting waste causes swelling from inflammation that weakens the tight joints in the small bowel. This inflammation widens the space, and the tight joints loosen allowing incompletely digested plant proteins to slip into the blood stream between the cells of the intestinal wall. The protective system of tight joints is now leaking, hence "Leaky Gut Syndrome."

These plant proteins, called lectins, can cause

serious trouble. As lectins penetrate the protective barrier of the tight joints of the small bowel's protective lining, they are immediately recognized as trouble by the immune cells in

the blood. Antibodies are formed to fight these intruders. These plant proteins, however, share many common characteristics with our own body proteins. This is the link to autoimmune diseases traced to eating grain and beans.

Wheat germ agglutinin, for example, contains chains of amino acids nearly identical to those found in joint cartilage and myelin proteins found in our nerves' protective covering. The immune system now can mistake our cartilage for the wheat invader that was let in through the leaky gut, loose cell junctions. The body turns its protective power on itself, hence creating an autoimmune disease. Similar examples have been found in the eye, kidney, thyroid, insulin receptors, and insulin producing cells in the pancreas. Kidney beans, ironically, produce lectins that trigger antibody formation, which through mistaken identity attacks our kidneys.

Crohn's disease, ulcerative colitis, rheumatoid arthritis, ankylosing spondilitis, systemic lupus erythematosis (LUPUS), type I diabetes, multiple sclerosis, psoriasis, Hoshimoto's disease of the thyroid, glomerular nephritis of the kidney, and many other diseases are now positively linked to eating grains and beans, and lectins they produce. There is much evidence that autoimmune diseases did not exist until humans began to process and eat whole grain. Archeologist can track the spread of rheumatoid arthritis around the earth to a society beginning to eat whole wheat. Another example is found in multiple sclerosis, which occurs where wheat and rye are eaten, but not where rice is eaten.

In Europe, the diagnosis of another common problem caused by the gluten found in wheat frequently occurs. It is rarely diagnosed in America, but I suspect occurs just as frequently and is misdiagnosed by our doctors poorly trained in nutritional diseases. This disease is called celiac sprue.

I have recommended to my patients that they look at their food choices based on their family history. If they have a family history of any of the autoimmune diseases; they should perhaps exclude all grain from their diet. If you eat a diet heavy in grain, you are probably weakening your tight joints in the small bowel and it might just be a matter of time before you develop one of these serious diseases. If you already have one of these diseases, I would suggest eliminating all grain from your diet. I have found that reduction of grain in anyone's diet helps relieve gastrointestinal reflux disease (GERD) within weeks and many other "tummy troubles" magically go away.

Lastly, let's talk about the addictive nature of grains. They literally are "feel good" food. This factor encourages us to eat more and more grain in order get the same high we got the first time we ate it. Grains have actual drug-like substances called, opiod peptides, that create a true addiction. Remember that heroin comes from the grain of the poppy plant! Eating grains will promote a sense of comfort and often a euphoric feeling. When we go "on a diet," we stop these foods. An overwhelming craving eventually occurs as we withdraw from the effects of the substance and we often will binge or "pig out" on the forbidden food (drug), just like any addict.

Most Americans eat grains every few hours without even thinking about it. Grain foods are handy, cheap, and give us a renewed high as the previous grain begins to wear off. To make things worse, the grain is usually combined with sugar. This also cause peaks and valleys of our blood sugars with this high glycemic load food (see Appendix II) that complicates the insulin regulation in our body.

The food manufacturers think in terms of best selling products. This usually means the most addictive products. Did you know the largest grain food producer is Phillip Morris? They own Kraft Foods, Nabisco, Post Cereal Company, and others. They are changing their food division name to Altria which comes from the Latin root *altus* which means "high." There are now amusement parks owned by Kellogg's and General Mills. Our children develop brand awareness early and probably become loyal consumers (addicts) for life.

Now I once again ask if grain is meant for survival food or everyday consumption? Only you can decide for yourself and the ones you love.

The Omega Fatty Acid Ratio Is Killing Us........

Recent Medical Articles

Cholesterol and Lipids in Mental Illness

"Omega – 3 fatty acids in bipolar disorders"
Marlene Freeman, M.D. et al <u>Archive of General Psychiatry</u> 56
(May 1999) pp407-412

"Omega – 3 fatty Acid levels in the diet and red blood cell membranes of depressed patients" R. Edwards et al,
<u>Journal of Affective Disorder</u> 48 (March 1998) pp149-155

"Lowered omega – 3 polyunsaturated fatty acids in serum phospholipids and cholesterol esters of depressed patients"
M. Maes et al, <u>Psychiatry</u> (March 22, 1999) pp175-191

We humans spent hundreds of thousands of years eating a diet loaded with fat. We only began eating grains about 10,000 years ago. In 1910 we consumed 83% of our fat as animal fat and 17% as vegetable fat.

Where do our calories come from today?

White bread, rolls, cereal, crackers, doughnuts, cookies, sodas, fruit juice and cakes….. The majority are made of cereal grains and processed fats never eaten by hominids or humans for 99% of our existence on the face of the earth.

Fats are very confusing to most of us. It is easier to just eat no fat, than try to figure out the good, bad and the ugly!

<u>Saturated Fats</u> basically come from animals and dairy.
(Butter and Lard)

<u>Monounsaturated Fats</u> come from some vegetables, poultry and nuts.
(Olives, Nuts, Poultry Fat, Lard, Avocados)

<u>Polyunsaturated Fats</u> include what we call essential fats, because they must be eaten and are essential to our health as well.

Omega – 3

Omega - 6

Omega – 3   (DHA and EPA) come primarily from cold water fish that feed on plankton. It is also found in flax, fig and raspberry seeds. It takes almost ten times as much flax seed oil, however, to equal the same amount of useful Omega 3 as fish oil.

Omega – 6 comes from vegetable oils, grain, and arachadonic acid from egg yolks and red meat.

These polyunsaturated fats make the cell membrane flexible.
The more supple and flexible the cell membrane, the more insulin sensitive the receptor sites. (See the Insulin chapter)

These essential polyunsaturated fats (Omega –3 and Omega – 6) are transformed into Eicosanoids. <u>Eicosanoids</u> are the most biologically active of all substances in the body. They are intercellular, so you can't detect them in the blood.

They act on most functions in our body like the accelerator and brakes on a car. They are the ying and yang of our physiology.

The two types of eicosanoids are required to work in concert in order to achieve fine control of various psychological and physiological processes.

Omega – 6

- Cause the blood to be more prone to clot.

- Promote rapid growth of cells.

- Induce smooth muscles cells to contract.

- Bring about an inflammatory response.

- Cause pain.

Omega – 3

- Blood Thinner

- Slows the growth of cells

- Relaxes smooth muscle contractions

- Anti inflammatory response

- Relieves Pain

- Replaces and repairs the nerves and brain.

Ancient Hunter Gatherer Diet
Ratio Omega 6 to Omega 3

2 : 1

Typical American Diet today

20-50:1

Remember Omega –6 eicosanoids are the ones that cause pain, inflammation, smooth muscle contractions, blood clotting, etc.

Remember Omega – 6 are found primarily in seeds, which means grain and grain products.

Omega-6 : Omega-3

Grain fed beef meat is a ratio of 15 : 1

Wild game meat is a ratio of 2:1

Grass fed beef meat is a ratio of 2:1

Increased levels of Omega 6 in the diet is directly linked to increased heart disease, insulin resistance, cancer, diabetes, neurological diseases, and accelerated aging.

Trans Fatty Acids

Today we eat another kind of fat that is totally artificial. Science has created liquid fat out of solid fat by injecting hydrogen atoms into the fat molecule. These fats are usually identified on the label of foods as "Partially Hydrogenated Oil".

They have a long shelf life. They are stable. They are sold in a clear glass bottle. They make lots of money for the manufacturers. They are deadly.

They replace the good Omega 3 and 6 and olive oil with a plastic artificial spread. In the past we thought they were heart healthy and all gave up butter and ate margarine. We gave up lard and used corn oil and safflower oil. We made a mistake. Here are just a few of the known problems with trans fats.

1. Lower HDL (good cholesterol)
2. Raise LDL (bad cholesterol)
3. Decrease Testosterone
4. Increase production of abnormal sperm
5. Decrease amount of cream in breast milk
6. Weaken the immune response
7. Increase the production of free radicals
8. Decrease response of insulin receptors
9. Cause hyperinsulinemia

You will find the highest levels of trans fats in bakery goods, in
sandwich cookies, in vanilla wafers, in animal crackers, and in honey graham crackers! This is what we are feeding our children's brains.

STOP IT!!!!!!!

Your brain is 60% fat, and the rest is cholesterol and protein.
Do you want to repair it with "Plastic Fat"?

The following diseases have been associated with fat problems in the brain.

- Depression
- Memory loss
- Violence
- Bi-polar disease
- Schizophrenia
- Alzheimers
- Multiple Sclerosis
- Parkinson's Disease
- ADD and ADHD
- Learning Disabilities
- Behavior Problems

OUR FOOD IS MAKING US CRAZY!!

My recommendation is that you
1. use no trans fats
2. use a pharmaceutical grade fish oil daily
(Omega 3)
3. decrease Omega 6 by limiting grain
4. use olive oil whenever possible for cooking
and salads

Pharmaceutical grade fish oil is not the kind you buy at a vitamin store or discount store or corner drug store. It is approximately $25 for a bottle of 100. It will not poison you with mercury, dioxins, and PCBs from the contaminated fish.

It takes approximately 100 gallons of health food store cheap fish oil to make 1 gallon of pharmaceutical grade. Price is the best indication you are getting the real thing. There are books in Appendix I, which will serve to guide you in this most fascinating chapter of nutrition.

Making Sense Out of Fat and Cholesterol....

Nothing in the body can be studied in a vacuum. Everything affects everything else. If you have not or do not read the chapter on Insulin and Glucagon, you will not understand cholesterol.

Exercise is also part of the cholesterol picture. We must, therefore, look at the whole body to try to understand its health.

There is "Good" cholesterol (HDL). There is "Bad" cholesterol (LDL). But did you know there is "Good" "Bad" cholesterol? That's right. Not all LDL was created equal.

What about "total" cholesterol? What are the triclycerides?

It is very confusing!!!!

What about all those drug ads on TV that show people ready to die because their cholesterol is above 200? Can you get it down with diet? Do you want to get it down may be a more important question?

Here is my opinion after doing my research of the literature. Don't go off your medication without discussing this with your doctor. Remember, opinion and fact often are the same thing in the mind of the person you are talking to, regardless of the letters after their name. Doctors give their opinions every day to patients and sometimes do not recognize where opinion and fact end and begin.

First we were told in the multimillion dollar campaign of the government and medical-pharmaceutical industry that cholesterol killed and was the problem with our health and in particular heart disease. We were told to eat low or no fat and to swing our diet to complex carbohydrates and whole grains.

It didn't work. In fact we got depressed and fat and autoimmune diseases increased. Heart disease didn't even decrease in occurrence. Heart disease actually increased. (It is unfair to draw any cause and effect relationship from this.)

In despair, blaming patients of being "noncompliant," doctors started patients on cholesterol lowering drugs. These drugs were not only expensive, but also had many side effects. As our testing of cholesterol became routine, we found that 40-50% of all adults in America had elevated cholesterol (as we <u>lowered</u> the normal values).

Since we all have cholesterol, and every cell in our body makes it, is it possible that we have misunderstood cholesterol? That really is a revolutionary thought! Cholesterol naturally occurs in all of our bodies. Why would it suddenly get out of balance in the 20th century?

Here are some "FACTS."

1. Cholesterol is NOT a fat. It is actually a waxy alcohol!
2. Every cell in the body has the ability to make cholesterol, but most is produced in the liver.
3. Only 20% of your body cholesterol comes from your diet. 80% is made in the liver!
4. You must have cholesterol to repair and replace the cells in your body. You must have cholesterol to make the cell membranes.
5. Cholesterol renews your body every day. You must have cholesterol to replace hair, nails, skin, the lining of your intestines every four days, muscle and even bone.
6. You must have cholesterol to produce estrogen, progesterone, testosterone, DHEA and cortisol….. all of the hormones!
7. It is the natural selective serotonin reuptake inhibitor (SSRI) in our brain. (This is what Prosac, Paxil, Zoloft, and Effexor do)

So what happens if we artificially drive down the cholesterol level in our blood stream with medications? Since cholesterol renews your body and makes it young, will we age prematurely with lowered cholesterol levels? Will lowered cholesterol actually cause harm in the long run? Will it cause depression? Will it cause decreased desire to be intimate or perform? I don't know, but the questions must be asked once we know that cholesterol is essential for life.

Because cholesterol is an alcohol, it cannot be carried in the blood stream. The water-soluble carriers are the lipoproteins: HDL (high-density lipoprotein) and LDL (low-density lipoprotein) as well as VLDL (very low–density lipoprotein) and IDL (intermediate-density lipoprotein). The HDL is almost all cholesterol and protein. The others have varying amounts of cholesterol, triglyceride (a true fat) and protein. The cholesterol is structural and the triglyceride is energy fuel.

1. <u>Total Cholesterol</u>: Is the sum of all the different types of lipoproteins with cholesterol. Unless it is really high or really low, it doesn't tell you much about your heart health.
2. <u>HDL Cholesterol</u>: There are now 5 subclasses, but it is the waste cholesterol from the cells, which is taken back to the liver to be excreted in the bile or recycled. This is the good cholesterol and can be as high as it can go without harm. You can

increase it by eating good Omega 3 fats and exercising and eating or drinking red grapes in all their forms.

3. <u>LDL Cholesterol</u>: Its job is to take the cholesterol to the tissues for their use in repair and rejuvenation. The problem is that it sometimes unloads on the vessel walls instead at a target organ and this forms a plaque. This dumping of cholesterol with plaque formation seems to be related to inflammation, oxygenation of LDL and carmelization (glycated) of blood sugar onto the LDL. Keeping your blood sugar stable, taking antioxidants (Vit. C, E, coenzyme Q10), alpha lipoic acid, nitric oxide and good nutrition seem to all decrease the risk of plaque formation. Most important is the fact that the number you get for LDL from your lab is not really a measure of LDL.

LDL cholesterol = the total cholesterol minus the HDL minus the triglycerides divided by Five

Even more confusing is the fact there is good "fluffy" LDL and bad "dense" LDL.

4. Triglycerides: Three fatty acids attached to sugar. It is the fuel the body loves to run on. It is stored as cellulite, spare tires, love handles, and beer bellies. It is also stored around internal organs and in your muscles. A high triglyceride puts you at the most risk for a heart attack.

Most of us feel the most predictive test for heart health other than hs CRP (see the chapter on this), is the triglyceride level divided by the HDL. This number should be 5 or less for optimal health.

This is a very, very simplistic approach to cholesterol and it is much more complex. I think the chapter on cholesterol in Michael Eades' book *Protein Power Lifeplan,* is one of the best discussions I have read. He also explains the many studies that have been unable to show that low cholesterol lowers risk of cardiac mortality from a heart attack. The people who do the best have total cholesterols of 160 to 220. Cholesterol less than 140 was actually as bad as above 240.

And lastly, remember that 50% or more of people with heart attacks have NORMAL total cholesterol.

The "statin" drugs are given to lower cholesterol. They have serious side effects as well. By controlling your blood sugar with a diet lower in grain, starch and sugar, and eating a good quality fat (Omega 3 and Monounsaturated) and having antioxidants and nitric oxide producing supplements in your diet, you may control the LDL and raise your HDL while lowering your triglycerides. That in essence is what you really want.

There is one other action of cholesterol, which we must not forget. It is essential to brain function. Numerous articles confirm that low cholesterol causes depression, rage, panic attacks, and other alterations of mood. Could our epidemic of mental illness be linked to our fixation on low cholesterol? Here are a few examples of studies from "real doctor" journals.

"Plasma cholesterol and depressive symptoms in older men"
Ross E. Morgan, et al <u>The Lancet</u> 341 (Jan. 9, 1993) pp 75-79

"Rapid decrease of serum cholesterol concentration and postpartum depression." Barbara Ploeckinger, et al <u>British Medical Journal,</u>(Sept. 14, 1996)   p 664_

"Low cholesterol level in patients with panic disorder: the association with major depression." M.Y. Agargun et al <u>Journal of Affective Disorders</u> (1998) 59L28032

There are those who contend that

"An egg a day keeps the blues away!"

Inflammation: Key to Illness........

Heart disease, arthritis, diabetes, cancer, asthma, allergies, osteoporosis, aging, alzheimer's disease, migraine headaches, fibromyalgia, periodontal disease, sinusitis, irritable bowel syndrome, thyroiditis, inflammatory bowel disease, chronic fatigue syndrome, metabolic syndrome, and senile dementia are all related to the silent epidemic destroying our health. It is also part of the process that damages our body tissues in multiple sclerosis, rheumatoid arthritis, systemic lupus erythematosus, and other autoimmune diseases.

That epidemic is inflammation. Inflammation is the most powerful concept in disease prevention and treatment today. It may indeed be the single phenomenon that holds the key to sickness and health.

As part of our immune system, inflammation is one of the most basic human responses to dangers, challenges and foreign influences on our health and life. Redness, pain, heat and swelling are all signs of inflammation. Every fever, bump, rash and bruise is a result of our body trying to protect itself from danger. When controlled and in response to trauma or infection, this inflammation can be life saving. When out of control and severe or long-term, it can kill us.

We have been treating inflammation since the dawn of man. We have only begun to understand it in the last 40 years.

Inflammation is not disease specific. It affects

the entire body, not just individual parts. Inflammation tells us that caring for our health means more than just caring for individual body parts. Scientists now know there are connections between gum disease and heart disease. Diabetes and thyroid disease are connected. Obesity is linked to depression, and insomnia is linked to chronic fatigue syndrome. When we treat inflammation in one part of the body the whole body gets healthier. The same inflammatory factors that cause heart attacks are suspected to cause strokes, diabetes, gum disease, premature births and many other seemingly unrelated disorders.

Dentists now refer patients with gum disease to cardiologists to prevent heart attacks! Doctors now understand that a simple blood test that measures inflammation, high sensitivity C-reactive protein, is the most important test that can be ordered on their patients. The widely prescribed drugs called "statins," are used to treat atherosclerosis and they work by decreasing and controlling inflammation. Why do you think an aspirin a day controls many risks of disease? Aspirin decreases inflammation as well as thinning blood.

So inflammation is both good and bad.

Remember the first and foremost role of inflammation is to protect the body and keep you alive.

So what determines how well our bodies keep inflammation in balance? Inflammation is influenced by what we eat (omega 6), over and under exercising, the pollutants we breathe, the toxins in the cleaning products we use, the insecticides and fertilizers we use, the amount of sleep we get, how much stress we experienced, the intensity of our emotions, and the quality of our social relationships. In other words, everything we eat, breathe, think, feel and do has an effect on our body's inflammation level!

So who needs to worry about inflammation? We all do! We cannot eradicate inflammation from our bodies. The key is balance and appropriate inflammatory response.

There are a number of excellent books in the appendix for those who want detailed information, but let me share with you some strategies to change your inflammatory state for the better. They cost nothing and are truly lifesaving.

Dietary Solutions

Food is one of the most valuable tool for maintaining the inflammation balance in your body. By tinkering with our diets, we can reduce aches and pains and increase mental clarity, regain energy and lower the risks for inappropriate inflammation.

Some foods are inflammation producing and some are anti-inflammatory. Our American diet is highly inflammatory, and that directly affects our incidence of heart disease, cancer, high blood pressure, stroke, diabetes, fatigue and depression.

The guide is simple:

1. Eat lots of fruits and non-starchy vegetables and greens
2. Eat wild caught fish 2-4 times a week or take pharmaceutical grade fish oil daily
3. If you use an oil, make it olive oil
4. Decrease or eliminate grain from your diet
5. Stop eating when you are full
6. Use daily supplements
7. Eat at home, not at fast food restaurants
8. Don't skip meals

Any change you make will help. Don't get

overwhelmed. For example, make a healthy lettuce wrap with a romaine lettuce leaf rather that a sandwich with bread.

Whole grain actually causes MORE inflammation than milled grain. Neither is good (see chapter "Going Against the Grain"), but try to minimize the bad effects. Remember that knowledge is power. Yes, I know. It tastes good to eat grain. Just be honest. You are supporting your drug habit and not feeding your health.

Building Solutions

They don't make buildings the way they used to and we are getting sick because of it. Windows used to open for fresh air. Now the air is sealed in and recirculated over and over.

Synthetic materials now make up carpeting, draperies, carpet pads, furniture, wall coverings and paints. Glues, adhesives, sealants, pesticides, cleaning products and air fresheners now surround us with chemicals. These changes have led to "Sick Building Syndrome" across America.

Respiratory infections are quickly spread, and a low level of chronic inflammation exists in all the people living and working in our closed, modern buildings. Fatigue, headaches, difficulty concentrating, memory loss, skin rashes, itching, muscle and joint pain have all been linked to these toxins. They are in our schools and daycare centers as well, where developing brains and bodies are "kept safe."

Now you see the advantage of fresh air. Despite the worries of air pollution outside, it is clear there is more risk inside than out. So, go for walks. Roll down your car windows when out of traffic. Open the windows of your house (even in the winter). Watch everything you spray and keep it away from your body. Even perfume may increase the inflammation in your body, not to mention deodorant and body creams and oils.

Lifestyle Solutions

People do not like anyone telling them how to live their lives.

I will just cut to the chase.

Here is the list:

STOP!

1. Smoking, Chewing or Snorting Tobacco
2. Drinking Alcohol
3. Cocaine
4. Marijuana
5. Promiscuous Sexual Activity
6. Excessive Calories
7. Lack of Exercise
8. Over Exercise
9. Tight Clothing

Here are ways to decrease inflammation.

1. Dressing in layers to control temperature and not get too cold or too hot
2. Moderate exercise with short duration high intensity or walking
3. Loving, Long Term Sexual Relationship

Wholesome sexual relations with a life partner decreases inflammation and increases well-being. Sexual activity increases the activity of the neurotransmitter dopamine. Dopamine is an anti-inflammatory and has been shown to suppress the inflammatory causing cytokine IL-12 while stimulating production of anti-inflammatory cytokine IL-10. Animal studies show that rats with higher levels of sexual activity have longer life spans.

Mind-Body Solutions

We can easily accept the relationship between toxins in our environment, food, alcohol and smoking and our health. These outside influences make the inside of our bodies change. It is more of a leap of faith to accept that we can create our own inflammation from within.

Our thoughts, stress, mood, feelings, and even our social surroundings can trigger inflammation in our body, which will just as surely lead to heart disease, pain, and even cancer. Every time you speak, read, ponder, move, dream, plot, or even daydream you are awakening neurotransmitters in the brain, which communicate with the body.

With every awakening of the brain, we release chemical messengers that have effects beyond our original thought.

The neurotransmitter serotonin is the modulator

of the "feel good" center of our brains. It is responsible for feelings of calm and happiness. People who don't produce enough or break it down too fast, have panic attacks or social anxiety or depression. The most frequently prescribed class of drugs today in America are SSRIs. That stands for Selective Serotonin Re-uptake Inhibitors. Paxil, Prosac. Sarafem, Zoloft, Effexor are all drugs which help keep the serotonin levels up. They treat depression and other conditions related to a serotonin imbalance.

These drugs are almost given out with every visit to a primary care giver in America today, because the number one complaint in a doctor's office is fatigue. The primary care giver has been well educated by the pharmaceutical representatives that the number one symptom of depression is fatigue. Hence one more prescription is written for an SSRI.

The relationship between the imbalance of neurotransmitters and alterations of mood have been known for decades. The knowledge of the effect of depression, anger, anxiety, and stress on inflammation related chemicals is new.

We now know that when we have extreme emotions, they change our immune system, cardiovascular system, gastrointestinal system and endocrine system as well. That delicate balance between inflammation and anti-inflammation is lost. Certain inflammation-related chemicals are thrown out of harmony. An example would be the production of interleukin-6, one of the major inflammatory producing cytokines, which skyrockets with anger and rage as well as stress.

There is an epidemic of depression today, which is discussed elsewhere in this book. This just magnifies the epidemic of inflammation-caused illness. We all feel sad or blue once in a while. That is normal. We are not zombies, who have no emotions. We need to let those feelings out. We were designed to cry. Yes, even men were designed to cry. This is not a sign of weakness. It is a sign of humanity. It is a sign of humanness!

Here is what seems to be fact today about depression.

1. There are elevated levels of inflammatory cytokines in people who are depressed.

2. Giving antidepressant medications lowers blood levels of certain cytokines in depressed patients.

3. When giving cytokines to treat Hepatitis C and other diseases, we induce depression.

4. People with inflammation-induced diseases like diabetes, heart disease and autoimmune diseases have a higher level of depression than the healthy population.

5. Animal studies where cytokines were given to rats produced the symptoms of depression.

6. Decreased levels of cholesterol, as well as Omega –3 fats, are associated with depression.

The take-home message is that the human body and mind are inseparable and extremely complex. We do not understand even a fraction of the laws which govern our body and mind function. What we are seeing is overwhelming evidence that we have a system out of balance and out of function.

Psychological stress is probably the biggest risk factor for inflammatory disease we face. All inflammatory disease is increased by stress. So how do we relieve this risk factor?

1. Intense exercise of a short duration with release of Beta-endorphins and other feel good chemicals
2. Pilates exercise
3. Yoga
4. Meditation
5. Personal Development
6. Cognitive behavior therapy
7. Hypnosis
8. Medication
9. Vacation
10. Change jobs
11. Move to a new location
12. Get a fresh start
13. Music
14. Hobbies
15. Get a pet

Positive Emotions are all generated from within. There are many relaxation techniques. Find one you like. Progressive muscle relaxation involves tensing and relaxing individual muscle groups. Meditation done to a single repeated word, "one." Guided Imagery where you close your eyes and transport yourself to a pleasant location of your dreams. Deep breathing from the diaphragm can be done anywhere and anytime that stress is overtaking your emotions. And last but not least, there is laughter. Laughter is good for the soul and is an anti-inflammatory! Seek out joyful friends and associates. Bring laughter into your life as often as possible. And finally, learn to laugh at yourself and lighten up. As my kids used to say: "Chill out, Dad!"

Medicine

An ounce of prevention is worth a pound of cure. So what about the wonder drugs of today? It is my opinion that no medicine is as good as education and action to correct lifestyle and "mindstyle!"

Having said that, your doctor will treat the symptoms of inflammation with drugs. That is what doctors do. You now understand why an aspirin a day seems like a miracle cure. This topic is so important that you will find an entire chapter devoted to it and "Inflammation Medication" will answer most of your questions.

The Anti-Inflammation Solution

So what is a person to do? People who don't smoke, eat right and exercise still die! In America the cause of death is usually heart disease. What we are dealing with in life is risk. There are no guarantees when it comes to health and life and death. None. But there are risks and we can reduce those risks with knowledge. What is good for one person regarding inflammation may actually be bad for another. We are unique individuals.

Armed with a little knowledge you can understand the concepts and begin to reduce inflammation in your body today. Take a deep breath. See, you just did it. However, the oxygen you got in the breath is causing formation of free radicals, which will increase your chance of DNA damage, which may lead to cancer and your death! See? It is not simple! It is all very complex! This is not a machine we are talking about.

Our body is a living, breathing organism with an organization beyond man's understanding.

The good news about inflammation is that it is never too late to start decreasing it in your body. Once inflammation has caused permanent damage, such as joint destruction in rheumatoid arthritis or kidney failure in inflammatory disease of the kidney, there is no turning back. It is important to make changes now before that permanent damage takes place. Even after the damage has occurred, you can decrease pain and improve quality of life by decreasing inflammation.

So my counsel to you is to learn to enjoy the natural wonder of your body. Just look at your hand. How it moves. What it feels. How it grasps. It is one of the true wonders of all of nature and brought us to where we are today.

Protect that hand and your body by taking steps today to reduce inflammation. It could mean the difference between life and death.

C-Reactive Protein: The Master Test.........

Half of all heart attacks occur in people with completely normal cholesterol levels.

In fact, people with very low cholesterol have four times the chance of dying from their heart attack than those with high cholesterol.

One hundred percent of people who have heart attacks have elevated C-reactive protein tests. So what is this test?

We now know that measuring the level of inflammation in your body is even more important than your cholesterol. This is done by measuring the concentration of a protein that is released as a part of the inflammatory process. This C-reactive protein is produced in the liver during episodes of acute inflammation. It is part of the body's basic emergency response system.

When you get an injury or an infection, the immune response breaks down the injured and dying tissue to make way for new healthy tissues. This produces heat, redness, and swelling. The problems occur when this system gets out of control. Too intense an inflammatory response causes problems throughout the body.

We now know that inflammation is always present in the walls of the blood vessels of heart attack patients, even if they have normal cholesterol. This is the current understanding of the events leading to that heart attack.

In these patients, plaques don't build up on the inside of artery walls, blocking blood flow; instead, they grow into the vessel wall, pushing it outward. The artery stays wide open and does not show up on X-Ray studies of the heart vessels. These plaques are deadly because of their potential to become unstable and explode from trapped inflammation.

Whether the cholesterol plaque is simply blocking the artery or has grown into the wall, pushing it outward, our immune system responds in the same way. It sends special white blood cells to attack the plaque that has formed in the artery wall. All this immune cell activity triggers the liver to make C-reactive protein, which joins in the attack of the plaque. As these immune white cells arrive at the artery, inflammation occurs and this creates plaque growth and makes the plaques unstable. The plaque then can burst from the pressure of the inflammation and the damaged tissue under the plaque releases chemicals that make our blood clot. This results in a heart attack or even a stroke.

Recent studies have showed that C-reactive protein may even cause the original inflammation in the vessel wall with subsequent plaque formation as the vessel tries to protect itself from the inflammation. C-reactive protein, therefore, may actually trigger the formation of the clot and the subsequent heart attack. C-reactive protein can even cause cells in the artery wall to produce an enzyme that causes clot formation and delays breakdown of blood clots.

Fat cells produce C-reactive protein as well, and that seems to explain increased diseases in obesity related to inflammation.

I think one of the most important finding has to do with the predictive value of C-reactive protein levels in the blood. You can actually predict when a person will have a heart attack based on the values. We can also follow the levels as we intervene with anti-inflammatory therapies.

Critics of the test claim it is not specific to the heart but elevated in many diseases. My answer to that is "Of Course!"
In the chapter on inflammation, you learned that it is at the heart of most serious diseases in the body. If your C-reactive protein is elevated, wouldn't you want to know so that you can begin to do the things you now know will decrease inflammation?

I recommend yearly testing for all my patients

over the age of 40 and earlier if they are at high risk for inflammation. I actually get monthly tests on those with extreme elevation in order to track the results of their anti-inflammation activities.

Here are the critical numbers when evaluating the test results for C-reactive protein:

Less than 1 milligram/liter (mg/L):

You have a very low risk of developing heart disease and other inflammatory diseases.

Between 1 and 3 mg/L:

You are at average risk.

More than 3 mg/L:

You are at high risk for developing heart disease and other inflammatory diseases.

More than 10 mg/L:

You will have a heart attack within 10 years or you have another severe inflammatory disease or an acute infection.

Please get your test done.

Inflammation
Medication.....

Diet, exercise, environmental factors, lifestyle
choices and emotional stress are all part of the
inflammation vs. anti-inflammation balance in
our bodies. Sometimes when it gets completely
out of control prescription medication is the
answer. There is no one answer for everybody.
This is where you and your doctor need to be in
close communication as the right therapy for you

is selected. The medications we discuss in this chapter are all ones which should be taken only with a doctor's supervision.

Nonsteroidal Anti-Inflammatory Drugs

Some of these are available over the counter without a prescription, but still should be taken with caution since they are unnatural and have serious side effects. One of them is related to thousands of suicides a year. They all reduce inflammation, relieve pain, and lower fever. Aspirin, naproxen and ibuprofen are familiar household names.

The most famous anti-inflammatory drug is aspirin. Since ancient times it has been used as a bitter tea made from willow bark. The salicin from the bark was very rough on the stomach and many people got ulcers and internal bleeding as they used it. By the late 1800s, scientists were making synthetic sodium salicylate. A few years later, the Bayer Company, from Germany, was making the aspirin we use today. It is acetylsalicylic acid, which is tolerated by the stomach much better.

In the late 1900s, new drugs were developed
that blocked the action of an enzyme called
cyclooxygenase (COX for short). COX enzymes
produced in the body pro-inflammatory chemicals
called prostaglandins (an eicosanoid). These Cox
enzymes however, helped heal the stomach as well
as increased inflammation. It was next found
that the COX-2 enzyme was the one involved in
increased inflammation and a new class of drugs
was born.

These selective COX-2 inhibitors were miracle
drugs known as Vioxx and Celebrex. They
controlled the pain, heat and inflammation
of arthritis, but with less stomach irritation.
However, after their release and widespread use,
they were found in some people to increase blood
pressure, and increase heart attacks.

One key factor that must be understood is that,
all the non-steroidal anti-inflammatory drugs
only relieve symptoms. They do not cure disease.
As soon as they are out of the body, the pain, heat,
swelling and inflammation return and continue
to worsen. The best action is still to treat the
root cause of the inflammation, not cover up the
symptoms.

Many studies show the beneficial effects of

aspirin on the prevention of heart attacks and strokes due to the anti-inflammatory effects, as well as blood thinning. All non-steroidal anti-inflammatory drugs have been shown to decrease the development of Alzheimer's disease as well. Once the disease is present, however, they do not seem to have any effect.

Corticosteroids

These are drugs based on the natural hormone cortisone. It is made in the adrenal glands, located above our kidneys. It suppresses inflammation, but also suppresses our entire immune system, making us more vulnerable to infections. In the 1950s doctors used these drugs to treat everything, but then the side effects became apparent. These potent drugs affected every tissue in the body and suppressed the normal function of the adrenal glands. They caused obesity, osteoporosis, moon faces, wasting arm and leg muscles, thinning of the skin, rise in blood pressure and accelerated atherosclerosis. Wound healing was delayed. Serious infections spread through the body. Psychosis and depression were common with long-term use.

In order to use these drugs you must be under

the close supervision of a doctor. Short tem use is
now the norm. These are still miracle drugs, but
must be used with utmost caution.

Antihistamines

These drugs block the effects of naturally released
histamine. Histamine is found in many parts of
the body, but acts locally or at specific receptors.
It is another neurotransmitter in the central
nervous system. It is found in cells in the intestine
and signals the release of stomach acid. It plays a
role in tissue repair and wound healing.

Antihistamines will treat allergic symptoms,
but will also cause sleepiness. The nonsedating
antihistamines (Zyrtec, Allegra, Clarinex, and
Claritin) are most popular today and do not cross
into the central nervous system.

Statins

This is a class of drugs that is used primarily to
lower cholesterol and the LDL bad cholesterol.
They however, block inflammation and this may
be the actual effect on preventing heart attacks
and atherosclerosis. They block the activation

of the endothelial cells that line the blood vessels and hence stop the first step in the development of inflammation in the blood vessel wall and subsequent plaque formation. They also lower C-reactive protein levels in the blood.

Early studies suggest that statins may also play a role in other inflammatory diseases like multiple sclerosis. This is an autoimmune disease where inflammation destroys the myelin sheaths of nerve cells. In mice, statins stop and reverse paralysis. Statins are now being used to treat Lupus and rheumatoid arthritis in some centers.

Everything in life has some risk, however. Statin drugs have side effects, which might include muscle weakness, pain, tenderness, and severe muscle damage. Very dark urine may be the first sign that muscle is breaking down. The breakdown product, myoglobin, is being removed through the urine.
Statins can also elevate liver enzymes, although true liver damage seems rare.

ACE Inhibitors

Angiotensins are chemicals produced in the kidneys that are involved with blood pressure.

ACE (Angiotensin Converting Enzyme) converts angiotensin into the bad chemical that raises blood pressure. This same ACE increases inflammation in the kidney, blood clotting and cell growth and death. We think that is why ACE Inhibitors decrease atherosclerosis and inflammatory diseases. These medicines are usually prescribed for blood pressure control, but may have more important overall effects.

Hormone Replacement Therapy

A woman's ovaries produce estrogen, progesterone and testosterone during her reproductive years. These sex hormones protect against degenerative diseases like osteoporosis and atherosclerosis. Once the production ends with menopause, the woman quickly becomes susceptible to heart disease and has the same risk as men. This was not true prior to menopause.

Naturally occurring estrogen has an anti-inflammatory effect throughout the body. Widespread use of hormone replacement had been common until 2002, when some conflicting data was released from a study called the Woman Health Initiative. This study did not use bio-identical estrogen and progesterone. It used horse hormones and synthetic progestin, not progesterone from Mexican wild yams. Unfortunately, we now don't know what caused what. This study showed 30% increase in heart disease in patients on these unnatural hormones and an elevation in C-reactive protein. Blood clots were also increased on therapy. On the other hand, cancer of the colon was decreased by 63% and osteoporosis was decreased by 34%. Death from all causes was the same for treated and untreated groups. However, most interesting was the fact that those on HRT had 22% less overall health problems compared to those on no HRT.

I am sad that the data from this study has made many women give up any consideration of hormone replacement in the future. I firmly believe that using bio-identical hormones is completely different that synthetic, foreign hormones. I hope women will keep an open mind and make the decision for themselves. There is no question that female hormones are potent anti-inflammatory. Don't women live longer than men?

Insulin and Glucagon......

The ancient Egyptians were the first to write of a new disease called diabetes, characterized by sweet urine. They did not make the connection with their new diet, heavily dependent on grain, and this change in urine.

It wasn't until the twentieth century that medical scientists made the connection with diabetes and grain. In 1889 an Austrian researcher discovered that the pancreas produced a substance that controlled blood sugar. He found that by removing the pancreas from a dog, it developed diabetes. Before that, medical experts, using evidenced based medicine, had pronounced that diabetes was caused by injury to the kidneys or diseases of the stomach, blood, nervous system or liver. Once again this is evidence of the lies we live by, based upon experts opinions passed on to the public as fact.

There was then a flurry of feeding ground up pancreases to diabetics with no effect on their disease. These were mostly people born with diabetes and not the adult onset type (type II diabetes) we see in epidemic proportions today. What was found, however, was some control of sugar with starvation and exercise. These unfortunate diabetics lived very short, miserable lives.

In 1921 Frederick Banting and Charles Best isolated insulin from the pancreas and injected it into a dog with diabetes getting results. In

1922 the first human was treated. Insulin has literally saved millions of lives since then. Today's diabetic can live a life almost as normal as anyone else.

Today with the epidemic spreading around the world of adult onset, insulin resistant, type II diabetes, we are drawn to study this hormone with as much intensity as in the 1920s. We now know that the proper level of insulin in our blood holds the key to many of the functions recently gone awry in modern humans.

We will discuss The Metabolic Syndrome and Hyperinsulinemia/Insulin Resistance Syndrome in a subsequent chapter.

Insulin is the primary hormone driving all of metabolism and therefore, influences every cell in the body. It has been implicated in diseases as diverse as heart disease, cancer of the colon, polycystic ovarian disease, infertility, gastroesophageal reflux disease, peptic ulcer, high blood pressure, elevated cholesterol and triglycerides, type II diabetes, and clotting problems.

The level of sugar in your blood stream literally spells life or death. It is critical that it not get too low or too high. Everyone has heard about the diabetic comas that can occur when the sugars get too far out of balance. Your body has a very dynamic way of producing just enough insulin to keep your sugar in a healthy range. Problems arise when this system gets out of control. Insulin is made in the pancreas and released when blood sugar is elevated.

Insulin works by pushing the sugar out of your blood stream and into the cells. This occurs through special cell membrane areas call insulin receptors. If these receptors are not sensitive to the insulin or resist its attachment, the insulin levels rise in the blood and it requires more and more insulin to drive glucose into the cells. Juvenile diabetics do not make any insulin and even though their receptors are fine, they have no insulin to push the sugar into the cells.

Besides insulin, the body also makes another powerful hormone called glucagon. Like most things in the body the balance of these two hormones is critical to our health.

The following list summarizes what insulin and glucagon do in your body. Insulin normally is released in response to you eating a carbohydrate while glucagons is released when you eat protein or fat. Both work on your blood sugar levels. Insulin lowers it and glucagon actually raises it when it is too low.

<u>Insulin</u>
(Released when you eat a carbohydrate)

Lowers Blood sugar

Increases the Storage of Fat

Stimulates liver's synthesis of Cholesterol

Glucose Decreases
Growth Hormone Release

Stimulates growth of arterial
smooth muscle cells

Increases Appetite

Makes Kidneys Retain Fluid

Shifts Metabolism into *Storage* mode

Glucagon
(Released when you eat Fat or Protein)

Raises blood Sugar

**By Converting Protein and Fat
into Glucose**

Burns Fat

Decreases Cholesterol Production

Increases Release of Growth Hormone

**Decreases smooth muscle cells
in vessel walls**

Makes Kidney release fluid

Releases fat from fat cells for energy

Makes dietary fats into ketones for energy

Shifts metabolism into a *burning* mode

Now you just need to look at these two lists before selecting a snack. Ask yourself what you want to have happening in your body in the next half hour! Unfortunately we do not eat that natural, perfect balance of fats, protein and carbohydrates nature once provided as we hunted and gathered our food. Lets look at just the sugar in our diet today and what a difference a hundred years can make.

The consumption of sugar has greatly increased in the last 100 years. In 1900 the average American ate two pounds of sugar a year. Today the average man, woman and child eats over 175 pounds of sugar! The teenager today takes in 75% of their calories in starches and sugars rather than fruit, vegetables, meat or milk. All grains and sugars become simple sugars once they are digested. Whole wheat bread ends up the same as a candy cane!

Some foods cause a quicker rise in the blood sugar level than others and hence an insulin spike is produced. This is the basis for the glycemic index, so highly touted by nutritionists. Check Appendix II to see the latest understanding of a newer and better concept called glycemic load.

Fructose from corn syrup is cheaper than sugar

and now is widely used to sweeten everything from soft drinks to bakery goods. It was thought to be better than sugar and less harmful. As with many things in life, the more you use something the more you learn about it. We now know that fructose gets into the cell without using insulin, but it causes insulin resistance. Fructose causes increases in triglycerides and LDL (the bad cholesterol), increases aging and wrinkling of the skin, damages our DNA and causes hypertension.

This may be one of the major nutrition changes of the last 100 years that has created the epidemics of the late twentieth and early twenty-first centuries. Even sucrose is half glucose and half fructose.

So what about the artificial sweeteners? The only question I would ask is if they are nutrition or a chemistry experiment. I am through with chemistry experiments in my body. Most importantly...

THEY DO NOT HELP YOU LOSE WEIGHT!!!!!

That is right. Malnutrition makes you gain weight. It is lack of nutrition that is making us fat, not anything else!!! Rats if given aspartame will actually gain weight over their littermates given identical calories. Nutrition, not starvation, will keep you at your optimal weight. (Read the chapter on obesity.)

Saccharin has been used for over a hundred years, but not as food. It was discovered in 1879 and produced by the paint company, Sherman-Williams, as an antiseptic and food preservative. Due to sugar shortages in the two world wars and the discovery that it was three hundred times sweeter than sugar, it was used as a sugar substitute. It also had no calories and fed the "Calories In, Calories Out" myth of weight gain and loss. The problem is that, it causes the release of insulin and leads to insulin resistance and high fasting insulin levels.

Cyclamates were the primary artificial sweetener in the 1960s in America. They were banned in 1970 with evidence of increased cancers in rats. Subsequent studies have not confirmed this risk and it has been in use in Canada and Great Briton for the last 40 years with no increases in cancer over America.

Aspartame or NutraSweet has been the

primary artificial sweetener since cyclamates were banned. It is two hundred times as sweet as sugar and has fewer aftertastes than the other sweeteners. It does have 4 calories per gram, which is the same as white sugar! The savings is in the fact that it takes $1/200^{th}$ as much aspartame to sweeten the same as sugar. Hence the calories are negligible. It does not raise insulin levels. Like everything that is suddenly used by millions of people, the real experiment began once it was put on the market in our food. The chemical composition is basically two amino acids joined together. The problem arises when the body breaks down the dipeptide molecule through digestion into methanol (wood alcohol) and formaldehyde. Methanol can cause blindness. Formaldehyde is known to cause cancer. The FDA was concerned and finally decided that the amounts were well below the toxic level and, therefore, safe for human consumption. Actually methanol is a byproduct whenever you eat fruit, fruit juice or vegetables as well.

Subsequent studies have shown more serious concerns over the use of this sweetener. It has been shown as a combination of amino acids, to cross into the blood stream through the tight joints of the small bowel, and from there it travels to the brain. It has been shown to actually excite the brain cells to the point of death! Anyone with the symptoms of mood swings, lack of memory, trouble concentrating, headaches or insomnia, may want to avoid all aspartame in their diet.

Stevia is a natural sweetener from a tree in South America. It does cause insulin release. Despite widespread use in Canada, and Asia, no know cancer risk or other problems have been found.

Sucralose or Splenda is six hundred times as sweet as sugar. It is unusual in that the body cannot digest it. Even though it can stimulate the taste buds like sugar, it is never digested! Since it never enters the body (just passing through), it does not affect insulin or blood sugar levels. This seems like the perfect answer to sweet but no side effects. We will just have to wait and hope nothing is found as millions use it around the world.

I still go back to my ancient ancestors who rarely had sweet foods other than dried fruit and honey. I believe that is where my DNA meant me to be when making food selections.

We know that insulin and glucagon are the key to many things in the body, but most particularly the control of blood sugar, fat storage and cholesterol production. Food selection determines which hormone is released and how much.

The take home message is that insulin is needed in the right amounts, but promotes obesity, high cholesterol and other problems when its levels remain high in the blood.

Read the chapter on insulin resistance to learn what you can do to naturally control your insulin and even reverse the insulin resistance that plagues the baby boomers and their children.

Syndrome "X" The Metabolic Syndrome: Curse of the Baby Boomers.......

A new epidemic is taking over the land. There are four conditions that qualify one for this new disease that did not exist 40 years ago when I was in medical school (or at least was very rarely diagnosed).

1. High Blood Pressure
2. Type II Diabetes
3. Elevated Triglycerides
4. Obesity

It is called Syndrome X, The Metabolic Syndrome, Hyperinsulinemia/Insulin Resistant Syndrome, Baby Boomer Birthright, and even Metabolic Xyndrome. Whatever you want to call it, it is a killer!

How does this insulin resistance occur? Remember when you eat a carbohydrate it is turned to a simple sugar in your intestine and allowed into the blood stream through the tight joints in the small bowel. The blood sugar rises and your pancreas releases insulin and begins to produce more. The insulin attaches to the insulin receptors on the cell membranes and the receptors are activated to pump the glucose into the cell, thus lowering the blood sugar level. If the receptors become resistant to the insulin and are not activated, the pancreas puts out more insulin to overcome the resistance and lower the blood sugar. The pancreas continues to put out insulin until it gets a response, and the blood glucose level drops to a safe level.

This elevated level of insulin in the blood acts on the rest of the body and produces all the other effects of insulin, including cholesterol production in the liver, storage of fat, etc.

Eating lower glycemic load foods (see Appendix II) will help reduce the insulin spikes.

The question is what has caused the receptors to get resistant to insulin binding in the first place? There are books written just on that subject alone. The honest answer is that we do not know. People who have not eaten high carbohydrate diets and then increase their consumption are at greatest risk. This is seen in the Eskimo, Apache and Pima Indians. From one of the healthiest people 100 years ago, they now have one of the highest incidents of metabolic syndrome and all four of its conditions.

Today 75% of American adults have some insulin resistance!
This coincides with 75% of adult Americans who are overweight. So how do you know if you have

insulin resistance and can you prevent or reverse it?

I think the simplest test is the measurement of the insulin level in your blood when you have been fasting for 8 hours. The value should be less than ten and the lower the better.

What if you already have insulin resistance or are worried about an elevated fasting insulin level? Here are the simple things you can do and they almost always work. I monitor patients by getting fasting insulin levels along with their lipids every two months when they are following this treatment regime. It all involves nutrition and getting the body back in harmony.

1. Decrease the consumption of grain and all starches.
2. Consume adequate calories, but not overeat.
3. Short duration, but high intensity, low impact exercise: the ROM machine, Pilates or yoga.
4. Decrease Omega 6 fats and increase Omega 3 fats.

5. Take supplements to replace the micronutrients we no longer find in our food.
6. Take Nitric Oxide releasing supplements at bedtime.
7. Eat lean protein daily and with every meal.
8. Eat fruits and vegetables and greens from a selection of lower glycemic load foods.

In my experience fasting insulin levels have gone from a high of 26 to 7 in 4 months just by supplementing and making these changes in food selection! Will it work on everyone? NO. The longer the insulin level stays elevated, the more permanent damage will occur to the pancreas as well as the insulin receptors. This is an area that needs to be addressed with your physician. Getting the diagnosis is extremely important and the fasting insulin level is the key in my experience.

Turning Back the Hands of Time.........

1905 vs 2005

The year 1905:

The year is 1905...one hundred years ago. What a difference a century makes!

Here are some of the U.S. statistics for 1905.

The average life expectancy in the U.S was 47 years.

The five leading causes of death in the U.S. were:
1. Accidents or trauma
2. Pneumonia and influenza
3. Tuberculosis
4. Diarrhea
5. Birth or birth complications

Only 14 Percent of the homes in the U.S. had a bathtub.
Only 8 percent of the homes had a telephone.

There were only 8,000 cars in the U.S., and only 144 miles of paved roads. The maximum speed limit in most cities was 10 mph.

Alabama, Mississippi, Iowa, and Tennessee were each more heavily populated than California. California, with 1.4 million people, was only the 21st-most populous state in the Union.

The average wage in the U.S. was 22 cents an hour.

The average U.S. worker made between $200 and $400 per year. A competent accountant could expect to earn $2000 per year, a dentist $2,500 per year, a veterinarian between $1,500 and $4,000 per year, and a mechanical engineer about $5,000 per year.

Ninety five percent of all births in the U.S. took place at home.

Ninety percent of all U.S. physicians had no college education. They attended medical schools or apprenticed with another doctor. The schools were not accredited, but were usually started by a famous doctor.

Most women only washed their hair once a month, and used borax or egg yolks for shampoo.

Canada passed a law prohibiting poor people from entering the country for any reason.

The American flag had 45 stars. Arizona, Oklahoma, New Mexico, Hawaii, and Alaska hadn't been admitted to the Union yet.

The population of Las Vegas, Nevada, was 30.

Crossword puzzles, canned soda pop and beer, white flour, and iced tea hadn't been invented.

There was no Mother's Day or Father's Day.

One in 10 U.S. adults couldn't read or write. Only 6 percent of all Americans had graduated high school.

Marijuana, heroin, and morphine were all available over the counter at corner drugstores. According to one pharmacist, "Heroin clears the complexion, gives buoyancy to the mind, regulates the stomach and the bowels, and is, in fact, a perfect guardian of health."

Well things have certainly changed! What hasn't changed is the quest for the fountain of youth. Ponce De Leon and his Florida exploration, and others too numerous to count have joined the quest. Today is no different.

"The Fountain of Youth"

The Baby Boomers are not about to grow old. They want to mountain bike till they die. "Long Term Care? What is that? Let me defy the ticking clock, and cheat the medical system of profits from my aging. I have always done it my way, and I'm not changing now! "

These are all thoughts that fill the minds of Americans born between 1946 and 1964. The Boomers make up 28% of America's population but have 50% of the spendable income. Their desire to cheat "Father Time" will make them vulnerable to the "Wellness Revolution" predicted by economist Paul Zane Pilzer. This will be a trillion dollar (that's 1,000 billion) industry by 2010, he predicts. So who do you trust with your body's future?

You will be bombarded from all sides, by people promising you whatever you want, in order to separate you from your money. Will there be legitimate products and treatments to turn back the clock? YES! How will you judge the value of the service? Ask to see their results. Ask to talk to consumers who have used their products or treatments. How long have they been in business? How long has the treatment been used? What are the side effects? Will you look younger while shortening your life?

Unfortunately, we will not know some of these answers for decades. Complications often don't

show up for years. That is why the best offense for age related disease is a good defense. Is exercise destroying your joints? Should you walk rather than run? Should you carry light hand weights for a long time rather than press huge amounts for a few seconds? What about tobacco, alcohol, drugs (prescription and street)?
Can we get "good" nutrition merely by eating "natural" foods?

Probably the number one prevention for aging is good nutrition. Seventy percent of all illness is diet related, but I didn't learn about this in medical school, as you now know. I learned more on the farms and dairies of New Mexico as a Senator. Cows live twice as long and produce up to four times as much, if given the right nutrition. But I'm afraid we feed our pets better than our kids. Farmers will spend upward of $250,000 per year for nutritional consultations for their cows. That's because it's good business. Cows are mammals and we are mammals. Vitamins and supplements probably are just as essential to our health today, as they are to cows on our ranches.

We no longer live in the Industrial Age. We live in the information Age. He who has the knowledge has the power, and as the futurist Toffler predicted 14 years ago, the power has shifted. Make knowledgeable decisions regarding your health. The key to aging will be discovered in the years to come.

Only by caring for your body now and not abusing it, will you have quality as well as quantity of life. But consumer beware! Go slow when making your decision on health. Use some common sense. Remember if it's too good to be true, it probably isn't true.

<u>NUTRITION:</u> THE KEY TO ANTI AGING

Was there ever a time when humans lived for thousands of years?

Did you know that there are 41 countries where people live longer than in America according to the World Health Organization?

Life Expectancy At Birth Ranking 2004

Andorra:	83.47	1
Macau:	81.69	2
San Marino:	81.23	3
Japan:	80.80	4
Singapore:	80.17	5

Australia:	79.87	6
Guernsey:	79.78	7
Switzerland:	79.73	8
Sweden:	79.71	9
Hong Kong:	79.67	10
Canada:	79.56	11
Iceland:	79.52	12
Italy:	79.14	13
Gibraltar:	79.09	14
Cayman Islands:	79.03	15
Monaco:	78.98	16
Liechtenstein:	78.95	17
Spain:	78.93	18
France:	78.90	19
Norway:	78.79	20
Israel:	78.71	21
Jersey:	78.63	22
Faroe Islands:	78.59	23
Greece:	78.59	24
Aruba:	78.52	25
Netherlands:	78.43	26
Martinique:	78.41	27
Virgin Islands:	78.27	28
Malta:	78.10	29
Montserrat:	78.03	30
New Zealand:	77.99	31
Belgium:	77.96	32
Guam:	77.94	33
Austria:	77.84	34

United Kingdom:	77.82	35
Saint Pierre:	77.77	36
Isle of Man:	77.64	37
Germany:	77.61	38
Finland:	77.58	39
Jordan:	77.53	40
Luxembourg:	77.30	41

United States: 77.26   42

Guadeloupe:	77.16	43
Bermuda:	77.12	44
Saint Helena:	77.01	45
Ireland:	76.99	46
Cyprus:	76.89	47
Denmark:	76.72	48
Taiwan:	76.54	49
Cuba:	76.41	50
Anguilla:	76.31	51
French Guiana:	76.30	52
Kuwait:	76.27	53
Costa Rica:	76.02	54
Chile:	75.94	55
World Average	63.79	155

The key to longevity is holistic. The key is
lifestyle as well as genetics. You cannot control

who your parents are, but you have total control of what you do with your genetics and how you live your life. Nutrition and physical activity are the variables you can control. I hope you agree by this point in the book that our food is killing us!

We talked about the causes of death in America throughout the book and especially in the chapter on death. So the solution is simple. Live in such a way that you escape heart disease, cancer, doctors, high blood pressure and diabetes! Remember:

70% of Doctor Visits are Diet Related

Deaths in America are Diet Related

Nutrition IS Good Medicine.

Then why don't doctors learn about nutrition in medical school? 55% of Adults are obese in America. There is a 100% increase in childhood obesity. There is a 70% increase in Type II Diabetes. There is a 10 fold increase in osteoporosis. These are all diet related.

So how do we change these dismal statistics and live longer and healthier lives? A change in diet is a change in life!

More than 9000 scientific studies have been conducted to document the effects of different types of food on our health.
They show that food is actually our best medicine (despite what I have said about "evidence based medicine")!

So what causes aging?

The number one cause is oxidation. Be sure and read the chapter on anti-oxidants for the details. Through "Oxidation" and the formation of "Free Radicals" we age even though we replace our entire body every seven years. This process is accelerated by the lack of "Anti-Oxidants" in our modern diet.

We eat almost 100% artificial food. Our food today, never occurred in nature except as a mutation of a normal plant or animal. Most of what we eat is a result of agriculture, animal husbandry, horticulture and bioengineering. That is why we must supplement our diets today. We must have all the food components every day for perfect cellular and even molecular nutrition.

Total Cellular Nutrition

Protein
Carbohydrates
Fats and Oils
Vitamins
Minerals
Micronutrients
Water

All day, everyday, for a lifetime.

I believe these ten foods can make you healthier and help you live longer:

1. **TOMATOES:** These are a major source of the strong antioxidant lycopene in our diet. Lycopene reduces the risk of cancer by 40% - notably prostate, lung, and stomach cancers - and increases cancer survival. Tomato eaters function better mentally in old age and suffer half as much heart disease. Concentrated tomato sauces have five times more lycopene than fresh tomatoes and canned tomatoes have three times more than fresh.

2. **OLIVE OIL:** It is a major part of a Mediterranean diet, shown to help reduce death from heart disease and cancer. Heart attack survivors on a Mediterranean diet had half the death rates of those on an ordinary low-fat diet, recent research shows. Olive oil, unlike other vegetable oils, is high in antioxidant activity. It is a monounsaturated fat.

3. **RED GRAPES:** This includes red grape juice and wine. Certain red grapes have moderate antioxidant power. However, purple grape juice tops other juices in antioxidant activity, having four times more than orange or tomato juice. Red wine has less antioxidant capacity than purple grape juice or green tea.

4. **NUTS:** These are one of our early evolutionary foods and ultra-compatible with survival. Recent Harvard University research found that eating more than 5 ounces of nuts a week cut heart attack deaths in women by over 40% and helped prevent deadly irregular heartbeats in men. Almonds and walnuts lower blood cholesterol. Nuts are high in fat, but most

is the good-type: monounsaturated and/or omega-3 fatty acids. Unsalted, fresh nuts are the best kind. They are one of the few natural foods still available to humans unchanged for thousands of years and are a must on your diet.

5. **SOY:** A new study suggests. middle-aged women who ate one serving of soy per day had a 15% lower death rates than women eating refined processed grains. When you look at the countries where people live the longest, the Asian diet, high in soy, ranks right up there with the Mediterranean diet. The news and some nutritionists have attacked soy recently as being unhealthy, but millions of Asians can't be wrong. Many studies in America show the selective estrogen receptor modulator (SERM) function of soy that seems to be an anticancer benefit that may account for the low prostate and breast cancer rates in Asian. I have no doubt that soy use will promote longevity. It is a grain, but no lectins have been identified from it that cause autoimmune disease or increased inflammation.

6. COLD WATER FISH: These contain high amounts of Omega-3 fatty acids that performs miracles throughout the body, fighting virtually every chronic disease known. Without it, your brain cannot think, your heart cannot beat properly, your arteries clog, and your joints become inflamed. You need at least an ounce a day or two servings of fatty fish a week. Both red and pink canned salmon, sardines, cod, white fish, mackerel, herring, and tuna are rich in the essential Omega-3's. Make sure you don't buy farmed fish which are fed grain (Omega-6).

7. BLUEBERRIES: One of the best antioxidant-rich foods. Blueberries are so powerful in retarding aging in animals that they can block brain changes leading to decline and even reverse failing memory. How much should be eaten? The human equivalent of the amount used in animal studies is a half-cup of frozen or fresh blueberries a day.

8. GARLIC: This herb is packed with nutrients known to help fend off cancer, heart disease, aging, and other health problems. Garlic has prolonged cancer survival time and extended animal lifespans by about 5%, which in humans might add about four years. Let crushed garlic "rest" about ten minutes before cooking it, to preserve its disease-fighting agents.

9. SPINACH: This super health-promoter is second among vegetables only to garlic in antioxidant capacity. It is also rich in folic acid, which helps fight cancer, heart disease, and mental disorders. In animals, it protects aging brains from degeneration. Folic acid may help prevent Alzheimer's disease. Both raw and steamed spinach contain high antioxidant and other essential nutrient contents.

10.   GREEN TEA: Green has a huge amount of antioxidants and incredible benefits. Harvard researchers recently found that drinking one cup of green tea a day cut heart-disease risk in half.

And then you still will need to supplement!

Physical Activity Is Also Vital To Long Life.

We were made to move.

Do what your ancestors did.
All movement is good.

Walk-Stretch-Breath-Carry-Throw-Bend-Rub

Exercise releases your own human growth hormone, when coupled with the right nutrition. Just don't over do it. There are only so many bends in an elbow or a knee. It does not have to hurt to help. "No pain, no gain" is for people into self inflicted pain and that is a form of mental illness.

So there you have the keys to a healthy and, hopefully, a long life. It is also important that it be a happy life. Happiness is extremely important. Stress increases oxidation and the release of free radicals and the subsequent aging of your cells. Have you ever noticed the difference between the face of a man elected president on the day of inauguration and the same man eight years later. You will see far more than eight years of change.

Spiritual peace is also essential to anti-aging. A good state of mind, a feeling of worth, and happiness with oneself are keys to longevity. Be anxiously engaged in good causes, volunteer and give of yourself for real peace. People involved in organized religion live longer in America.

Anti-
Oxidants......

We can't <u>live</u> without oxygen and we can't <u>die</u> without oxygen! That is a fact! We begin to die with our first breath!

Oxygenation occurs in our bodies just like it does everywhere else in our world. Cut an apple and leave half on the counter while you eat the other half and the remaining apple quickly turns brown as a result of oxidation. The patina on a copper or bronze statue is a result of oxidation. The rust on a car….. oxidation. The tarnish on silver…… .oxidation! When man oxidizes, we call it aging and sometimes cancer!"

Antioxidants counter this process.

We were given foods in nature for our DNA to cope with this oxidation. Those were foods we could get as a hunter-gatherer. It was the color of the foods that had the anti-oxidant that we could get as a hunter-gatherer.

Today we eat only 15 to 25 different foods. Our ancient forefathers ate 100 to 150 different foods. Their only restraint to variety was seasonal availability.

The rich variety of plant foods available to them gave enormous amounts of widely different antioxidants. Today the limited foods we eat are often purged of their antioxidants by processing.

It is the colors of the fruits and vegetables that hold the key to reversing oxidation. The chemicals that cause the color are the actual anti-oxidants. These are not the artificial colors added today to green, unripe fruits and vegetables sold in our stores as "fresh produce." It is the red in a ripe red grape that is good for your heart, not the alcohol in spoiled, fermented grapes called wine. It is the orange color in the carrot that helps the eye through anti-oxidant activity on the cones and rods located in the back of your eyeball.

Here are the seven color groups so brilliantly delineated by Dr. David Heber in his book "What Color is Your Diet?" Dr. Heber recommends one serving of fruits and vegetables a day from each of the seven different groups. The American Cancer Society also recommends multiple servings.

The Seven Food Color Groups

1. Red
Tomato juices, soups, or sauces, tomato, watermelon, pink grapefruit. Lycopene inhibits breast cancer cell growth in the laboratory.

2. Green
Broccoli, Brussel Sprouts, Cabbage, Bok Choy. Isothio-cyanates increase liver proteins that defend against carcinogens.

3. Green/Yellow
Spinach, corn, collard greens, kale, avocado, mustard greens. Lutein protects vision, the heart, and inhibits cancer cell growth.

4. Red/Purple
Grapes, strawberries, cranberries, raspberries, red apples, prunes, blueberries. Proanthocyanidins protect against urine infections. Ellagic acid inhibits cancer cell growth.

5. Orange
Carrots, butternut squash, cantaloupe, mangos, pumpkin, apricots, sweet potato. Beta carotene protects vision and immune function, and is an antioxidant.

6. Orange/Yellow
Oranges, lemons, pineapples, papaya, peaches, nectarines.
Flavonoids inhibit tumor growth and repair DNA. Limonoids in the skin of lemons and oranges inhibit tumor growth.

7.Green/White
Garlic, onions, pears, celery, chives, leeks.
Allyl sulfides inhibit tumor cell growth.

To really understand antioxidants, we must understand the "oxidants" against which they work.

When we breathe in oxygen, it goes to our lungs where it transfers into the blood vessels and is taken up by our hemoglobin in the red blood cells. The oxygen is then transported to the cells where it is released and used in the process of cell metabolism.

As we live and breath, we burn the food we eat for energy. This is done within the cell in an organ called mitochondria. As food is burned in these furnaces, an electron is released which an oxygen molecule eventually accepts, and ultimately water is formed as the waste.

The movement of these electrons releases energy that the cell uses for all its processes. In this process, some electrons escape and attach to atoms or molecules and convert them into "free radicals."

A free radical is an unstable molecule or atom with an extra electron. It only becomes stable by creating another free radical. It does this by transferring it's extra electron to another atom or molecule or stealing another electron from another atom.

A single free radical could damage many molecules before the chain reaction loses steam and plays itself out. Antioxidants step in and stop the chain reaction by accepting the renegade electron from the free radical. They are restored by other antioxidants to whom they transfer the extra electron and are available to work over and over again.

Sunlight, chemicals, toxins and our own immune system make billions of free radicals. The oxygen free radicals from breathing actually reach and damage the DNA inside <u>each</u> of our cells 10,000 times a day. Multiply that times 100 trillion cells, and you see the enormous number of free radicals produced daily in our bodies.

The free radical theory of aging, believes that it is the cumulative damage from years of free radical activity that takes it's toll, changing our cells, and causing us, over years, to have more and more abnormal cells and eventually die.

Remember that each day, each cell gets 10,000 hits to its DNA. DNA controls the replication of our cells. Damage to our DNA could cause a mutation and possibly the formation of cancer cells. These cells if not stopped, go on to form tumors, which take over our body and eventually kill us. It is the antioxidant "free radical defense team" that clips out the abnormal part of the DNA and prevents mutation of the cell. Without antioxidants we could not survive more than a few years, and we would be dying from cancer right and left.

The free radical attack on the lipid bilayer of our cell walls, is also a problem with aging. Free radical damage to the unsaturated fat causes the wall of the cell to be less supple and decreases its ability to function. Lipid peroxides cause the walls to become rigid. This leads to insulin receptor sites becoming resistant. Free radicals also cause the peroxidation of cholesterol, which leads to plaque formation in our blood vessels.

Remember, these free electrons called "Free Radicals" are released as part of the normal metabolic process and wildly bouncing off the adjoining parts of the cell damaging the DNA. This happens millions of times a minute, round the clock, in our bodies as long as we are breathing in oxygen. Just like the apple turning brown and the car rusting, we are oxidizing and beginning to die with each breath.

"Anti-Oxidants" from the color in fruits and vegetables as well as vitamins try to keep us alive by reversing the effect and repairing the damaged DNA while capturing the "free radicals."

NATURE IS AMAZING!!!!!!!!!!!!

I have made it sound simple, but in reality no one really understands the entire process. What we do know is that without antioxidants we age and die sooner. The logical leap is that with antioxidants we age slower and live longer. This is evidence based. It is based on the comparison of diets around the world and where people live the longest.

Unfortunately, the unripe, genetically engineered fruits and vegetables of today, with their artificial color, are just not as good as nature. They may actually taste better than natural vegetables sometimes due to the wonders of science, but this is an artificial taste. It is a drug experience, not a nutrition experience. Once again, here is evidence that we must supplement to give our bodies what nature used to do automatically. Does that make sense to you?

What I know is that, research done at Harvard Medical School and published in the *Journal of the American Medical Society (JAMA)* during the summer of 2003 came to the same conclusion.

Every adult in America needs to take supplements in order to prevent the major illnesses killing us today. Heart disease, cancer, high blood pressure, stroke, diabetes and even mental illness are all associated with our diet. Thousands of medical articles in "evidence based" doctor journals confirm this.

My recommendation is the same. I take antioxidants as supplements everyday. My family takes supplements everyday. I encourage my patients to take supplements everyday. In addition I do recommend fresh fruits and vegetables as close to nature as you can get. Local growers markets are the best source if you can not grow it yourself, but remember….. most seeds today are bioengineered and the result of science not nature. Once again we have evidence that we cannot purchase, at any price, our original natural food.

Supplementation for me and mine =

LIFE
Remember LIFE
is a Result of Nutrition.

Cancer: Cells that Kill.........

We all fear that someday we will hear the dread words, "I am sorry, but you have cancer." Cancer is the number two cause of death in America and spreading around the world. As the number of smokers declines, the most frequent cancers that kill are breast and prostate.

They are "brother-sister" cancers. In fact your risk is greatest if your spouse, not your parents, get their gender cancer. Perhaps it will make more sense if I tell you the foods linked with one cancer are also linked with the other. Do spouses eat similar foods? Do they live in a similar environment?

Similar numbers of men and women get these cancers. It is also interesting that the same diet that is good for maintaining weight and limiting heart disease and diabetes is good for the prevention and intervention of these cancers. Nutrition is emerging as one of the most important factors in preventing both breast and prostate cancer.

Two professors, Wael Sakr, M.D. at Wayne State University in Detroit and Gabriel Haas, M.D. from the State University of New York in Syracuse, did an important study which looked for microscopic cancer of the prostate in 600 men who died from any cause at any age. These were latent or dormant cancers.

They found it in 25% of men in their 30s.
They found it in 30% of men in their 40s.
They found it in 40% of men in their 50s.
They found it in 50-60% of men in their 60s.

They found it in 70% of men in their 70s.
They found it in 80% of men in their 80s.
They found it in 95% of men in their 90s.
There have been similar studies in women for the
microscopic incidence of breast cancer.

When the cancer occurs under the age of 50
in both men and women, it seems much more
aggressive and more likely to cause death and
spread quickly once diagnosed.

So half of us have these cancers as we enter
middle age. The majority of us have them as
we get into old age. That means that part of the
normal aging process is the universal formation
of cancer cells. Whether they become a tumor,

however, is dependant on where you live!

The risk of cancer is greater in some countries
than others.

The number of cells that go on to clinically
detectable tumors is 10 times higher in high risk
countries than in low risk countries. Even if a
tumor occurs in low risk countries, they grow
slower and are less aggressive.

Men in Japan and China have 90% less prostate cancer than men in America. Women in Japan and China have 90% less breast cancer than women in America.

When people move from a low-risk country to a high-risk country, the risk of cancer increases within 15 years. The reverse is true of movement from a high-risk to a low-risk country.

China has the lowest rate in the world of both cancers: 2.8/100,000 people. American Whites have a much higher risk: 100/100,000 people. This is 33 times the risk if you are a white in America than a Chinese in China.

Let us compare the Western and Chinese diet.

Western Diet

More Calories
Animal Fats
Red Meat
Food Preservatives
Starches

Chinese Diet

Less Calories and Fat
Green Leafy Vegetables
Pumpkin
White Meat
More Fiber and Fruits
Soy Beans

The change from the first cancer cell to a tumor is about 15 years for both breast and prostate cancer. Diet also has a significant effect after the cancer has already formed. Diet acts to inhibit cancer growth or stimulate cancer growth. Cancer growth can be slowed with as little as a 12% decrease in caloric intake at any stage of cancer!

Carcinogenic substances in our diet also include:
•Pesticides
•Chemicals in tobacco
•Chemicals used to smoke and pickle food
•Amines that form in cooked meats

These amines become carcinogenic due to enzymes in our immune system that are part of us being hunter-gatherers as we formed our original DNA.

243

Here are the nutrition high risk factors for cancer.

- **Animal Fat**
- **Obesity**
- **Lack of Fruits and Vegetables**
- **Lack of Micronutrients (antioxidant vitamins)**

The same dietary recommendations for prevention of prostate and breast cancer also protect you against heart disease, stroke, diabetes, other cancers and mental imbalance.

Probiotics are also needed to protect us. Over 100 Billion organisms live in perfect harmony in our bodies. Some strains stimulate our immune systems as growing children to give us healthy and strong bodies with good defenses. Others in our colon help breakdown fiber and other things we can't digest. They work to stimulate normal cell growth in the colon. Although not completely understood, lactobacillus, found in non-pasteurized cottage cheese, yogurt and buttermilk, seems to have a protective role for cancers and harmful infections.

Things are never simple, however.

The bacteria in our soil have changed and were a vital part of the lifecycle of the fruits, vegetables and animals that we originally ate. See, it is not simple. We have changed things we don't even know we have changed, and are now paying the price for messing with Mother Nature!

So how do we get cancer?

Cancer is another DNA disease!

Cancer can rarely be traced to a single gene inherited from our parents. Cancer most often is a result of complex interactions between....

- •Diet
- •Genes
- •The Environment

Cancer is a disease of "CIVILIZATION." It is not the same in all countries or societies, as you now know. Lets look at what happens on a cellular, even molecular, level.

"APOPTOSIS" is a big word for the life expectancy of every cell in our bodies. It is built into the cells when we are born. We have cells programmed to die at a particular time.

It is theorized that there is no cell in our body more than seven years old. Cancer becomes a tumor when the DNA mutates, possibly through oxygenation from breathing. The apoptosis is turned off. The cell does not die, but continues to reproduce and live. This creates a tumor of cells that are reproducing, but not dying.

Cells fail to die on schedule, and cancer cells can reproduce an unlimited number of times. The most at-risk sites of mutation are tissues where cells are replaced frequently throughout life.

- Skin
- Lungs
- Bladder
- Intestines
- Colon

High levels of hormone also enhance cell growth.

- Prostate
- Breasts
- Ovaries
- Uterus

Here are the steps that a cell mutation goes through.

1. Initiation
2. Progression
3. Invasion
4. Metastasis

Initiation

This is a mutation of one or more cells that begins the cancer. This is caused by the formation of "Free Radicals" by the oxidation of our food at the intercellular level. These "Free Radicals" bombard our DNA, damaging it. Anti-Oxidants repair the damaged sites. The body's defenses target the damaged cells and destroy them, or else they are free to reproduce and create a primary tumor. With increasing age comes more damaged DNA and hence more tumors.

Progression

The primary tumor cells continue to grow unopposed.

Invasion

The tumor next begins to grow its own blood vessels and invades neighboring tissues and interferes with organ function.

Metastasis

Next the tumor cells break off the tumor and travel through the blood stream and lymph system to organs outside the primary tumor site. They lodge there and continue to divide and take over new healthy tissue. Specialized proteins stimulate the growth of new blood vessels to feed these new tumor cells, and other proteins extend the invasion and metastasis into adjacent tissues. This process is very much like the process that happens when a fertilized egg implants in a uterus at the beginning of conception.

Genetic influences are quite complex and still not well understood. Extensive mutations continue and give a growth advantage to the tumor cells.

So in Summary:

Cancer is a DNA disease. Our genes come with us at birth.

We have no option to change them. Probably cancer is not inherited as much as it is a result of our environment and our diet. Oxidation through breathing and toxins in our environment and food create free radicals, which damage our DNA, causing mutations and shutting off pre programmed death of the cells. Unlimited cell division creates tumors, which eventually spread and take over the blood and nourishment of healthy cells until we die.

Cancer may possibly be prevented or even treated with a manipulation of our diet. This however is an "evolving" area of science and we should include it in our further study and understanding of how to prevent cancers in the future. We by no means understand the keys to prevention and treatment of the second most common cause of death in America today.

Mindless Aging.......

Who among us doesn't fear the loss of our mind and mental acuity, which is often associated with aging? Nutritional abuse, alcohol, drugs, mental laziness, and lack of mental challenges all add to the deterioration of our brains. Mental wellness is our genetic birthright, but we have learned to settle for less due to many misconceptions of inevitability.

The human brain is a marvelous organ that was designed to think, calculate, problem solve, and synthesize new and challenging thoughts and information. Just like your muscles, it will literally atrophy and die if it is not exercised on a regular and consistent basis. It needs to be worked to its limits and exercised frequently or it will lose even the level of performance it once gained. It will age and atrophy and even lose the neuro-connections it developed when young.

We daily have brain cells die, and they must be replaced with the good essential fatty acids, or the brain becomes corrupted and malfunctions and may even "break down." This is what all the concern over trans fats is about, which is bringing about new government labeling laws. It may actually save the brains of the next generation.

For those of us who are middle aged or beyond, our hope lies in activity and exercise of the brain cells and their connections. The key is a combination of the right brain nutrients to repair the daily losses and then to use your brain. All of, us regardless of age, need to use an Omega 3 fatty acid supplement. This is the fish oil or flax seed oil that are available to supplement our diet now so deficient in this critical building block of the brain. Our brain structure is 60-80% fat, and the rest is cholesterol and protein. It runs on glucose, but is mostly FAT. We are all fatheads after all. This must be pharmaceutical grade fish oil.

By changing the kinds of fats we eat, we have created an epidemic of learning disabilities, depression, and more studies are confirming schizophrenia, Alzheimer's, MS, Parkinson's, Lou Gehrig's disease (ALS), ADD and ADHD. We used to get the Omega 3 from eating the meat and brains of wild game and fish, but now we eat feedlot animals and farmed fish that no longer have the Omega 3s, but are filled with the Omega 6 fatty acid that doesn't fit in our brain structure. The ancient diet contained cholesterol that we got from eating red meat and eggs, which are on the "don't eat" lists today. Cholesterol is the naturally occurring SSRI which prevents depression. Medicine took away our cholesterol and now gives us antidepressants instead.

If we take dietary fat and cholesterol out of the diets of laboratory animals, they have mood changes that progress to depression, social withdrawal, and then aggressive behavior. Sounds like the stories on the nightly news! We have over 200 medical studies which show the level of cholesterol in the blood directly correlates with mood and behavior (in particular violence).

One study showed you are six times more likely to die violently from suicide, auto accidents or homicide if you have low blood cholesterol.

Lastly, we know that we can measure increased blood flow to the brain and nourishment with certain activities. Learning a new language, learning to play an instrument or even listening to certain music increased blood flow along brand new circuits and pathways in the brain and brought whole sections back "on line" as the brain was challenged to grow and stretch with the new activity. Just listening to an unfamiliar foreign language made the brain light up as it searched for meaning in the strange words! Studies also found that listening in particular to the music of Mozart improved concentration, released creative abilities, relieved chronic pain, and improved all intellectual activities.

So, we are beginning to unlock the keys to our brain, little by little, but we must stay alert to new ideals and resolve today to keep our brains working and not fall into routines of putting our brains on cruise control while sitting in front of a passive experience like TV.

A youthful brain can be a brain at any age that is used, challenged and not forgotten.

The Science of Aging Skin.........

Your skin is the largest organ in your body and it is truly a wonder. We take it for granted most of the time, but it is what allows us to live in any place on the face of the earth and regulate our internal temperature. It holds all the rest of us together and keeps the liquid in our cells.

Remember, we are mostly water.

Without skin we would be confined to live in a swamp and only a swamp that stayed the same temperature all the time. Skin helps us get rid of waste products and keeps out invaders that would otherwise kill us.

Our skin is also a reflection of our overall health. Have you noticed how animal breeders take care of the skin and hair and nails of their prize animals? You can tell by the sheen of the coat the health of the animal. You can tell by the glow of a cheek the health of a human.

Today, we cover up our skin so people won't see what we "naturally" look like. It is sad we don't have the nutrition to support the look we want. There is no way around the fact that skin care begins with nutrition. Protein, fats carbohydrates...... same story and same formula. Adequate protein to build new skin. Cholesterol is a must for healthy skin!!!!!!!!!

Besides nutrition the number one enemy of your skin is the sun and the radiation from outer space. All those different rays get a little confusing so let's see if we can make it logical. I have found in my lectures that an outline form seems to be most logical in explaining a very complicated organ.............. our skin.

UV Radiation and Free Radicals

Aging Skin versus Photoaging Skin:

Up to 90% of the visible skin changes attributed to aging are caused by sun exposure. Everybody, regardless of race or ethnicity, is vulnerable.

UV Radiation

UV rays have a number of harmful effects on the skin.
- There are two types
- The damage accumulate overtime
- UVA + UVB are linked to skin cancer
- UVB rays impact the surface of the skin
- Primary cause of sunburn
- UVA rays penetrate deep into the skin
- Both heavily contribute to premature aging

Ultraviolet B (UVB)

- Major action spectrum for both melanoma and non-melanoma skin cancer formation

- Most biologically potent in terms of overall short and long term consequences
- Responsible for the majority of tissue damage – resulting in wrinkles and aging of the skin
- Partially absorbed by the ozone layer
- Cause the common sun burn

Ultraviolet A (UVA)

- Penetrates much deeper (30-40x) into the skin than any other UV wavelength
- Can potentiate the carcinogenic effects of UVB
- Strongly absorbed by melanocytes – involved in melanin production and melanoma formation
- UVA contributes substantially to chronic sun damage and wrinkling

What is Causing This Damage?

FREE RADICALS!

- Oxidation, or the aging process of the cell, occurs primarily because UV light stimulates the production of free radicals

- Oxygen particles that have one or more unpaired electrons (unstable molecule)
- Produced by cells in your body as part of the normal life cycle
- They attach to healthy cells and steal away their positive electrons charge
- This action will eventually destroy the cell

Aging vs. Photoaging

Intrinsic Aging: Inevitably occurs as an organism progresses in chronological age.

<u>Chronological Aging:</u>

- Primarily occurs in the dermis
- Changes take place in the extra cellular matrix
- Skin naturally loses rigidity, elasticity
- More fragile and easily bruises or tears
- Higher incidence of skin cancer

Extrinsic Aging: Results from environmental effects such as UV exposure
- The biggest contributor to extrinsic aging is the effect of radiation from the sun (photoaging)

- Photoaging causes alterations in skin cell development
- Results in rough, leathery, wrinkled, sallowness and hyperpigmentation

Other Contributing Factors to Extrinsic Aging:
- Smoking
- Pollution
- Stress
- Alcohol consumption
- Extreme diets

The **GOOD NEWS** is we can transform damaged skin by addressing key skin cell functions! Let's look at the skin cell functions

Layers of Skin and Three Key Cells

The skin grows and renews constantly.

- Largest organ
- Barrier function
- Keeps "out" water and micro-particles
- Keeps "in" body fluids
- Grows and renews its self constantly
- Undergoes numerous changes
- Hormonal influences
- Illness, trauma

- Environmental exposure
- Process of aging

The Skin is divided into 3 layers
      11.   Epidermis
      12.   Dermis
      13.   Subcutaneous

Epidermal Layer

- Outer region of the skin
- Less than 1mm - width of a pencil mark
- Two key cell types
    1. Keratinocytes - keratin forming cells
       80% - 90%
    2. Melanocytes - melanin forming cells

These cells are organized into layers from superficial to deep.

The epidermal layer is subdivided into these layers.
- Basal layer – contains keratinocytes and melanocytes
- Spinous layer (prickle) – polyhedral shaped cells networked to form an intercellular bridge
- Granular layer – flatter cells, contain protein granules

- **Stratum corneum** - (horny layer) outermost layer of dead keratinized cells

Keratinocytes:

Are generated in the basal layer. Half of them remain there. They anchor the epidermis to the dermis. The other half differentiate from living cells to dead cells and travel toward the skin surface. When they reach the surface they exfoliate and are lost as peeling skin. They have a very important function to form the stratum corneum layer of dead cells that acts as the first line of defense as a barrier between our bodies and the environment. It normally takes 4 weeks (28 days) for the epidermis to replace itself. The dead cells stay in the stratum corneum for 12 days. This makes a total of 6 weeks for normal exfoliation of the epidermis.

Melanocytes:

They are interspersed among the basal keratinocytes. The melanosomes produce melanin pigment. Pigment granules are transferred to the surrounding keratinocytes. Variation in skin color is due to the number of melanocytes to keratinocytes, size, distribution of melanosomes, distribution of pigment granules and quantity of melanin produced. The melanin functions to maintain the skin color, provide protection from the UV rays and to shield deeper cells and tissue from DNA damage to the cell nucleus.

The Dermal Layer

- Undulating surface supports epidermis
- Provides nutrition and waste removal
- Connective tissue
- Collagen
- Elastin
- Natural hydration
- Subdivided into 2 layers: Papillary and Reticular dermis

Fibroblast

- Major cell of dermis
- Produces collagen and elastin fibers
- Controls turnover
- Collagenases
- Elastases

Dermal Layer

- Collagen fibers provide the skin with strength
- Elastic fiber network provides resiliency and elasticity
- Provide moisture through a sugar protein gel substance

- **Extracellular matrix controls the tone and turgor of the tissue and helps to resist compression**

Subcutaneous Tissue
- At the very bottom of the skin
- Formation and storage of fat
- Supports blood vessels and nerves
- Deeper hair follicles and sweat glands

Remember the skin is a living organ that can grow and renew itself constantly.

The key skin cells:

–In the Epidermis
- i. Keratinocyte
- ii. Melanocytes

–In the Dermis
- i. Fibroblast

The function of the Epidermis is form a healthy Stratum Corneum.

The function of the Dermis is to provide nutrition and structural support to the Epidermis.

So how does aging and damaged skin act?
Skin cell turnover significantly slows. Basal keratinocytes are producing abnormal cells. Melanocytes overproduce melanin and cannot distribute it evenly. The proper balance is not maintained between cell generation and cell loss. Weak connective tissue cannot support the epidermis with a strong framework and proper nutrient supply.

Here is how we repair and rejuvenate the skin.

We transform damaged skin cell functions to look and act younger by:

- Accelerate cellular turnover rate
- Reduce overactive melanocytes
- Repair intracellular transcription
- Stimulate fibroblast
- Increase angiogenesis (new blood supply and nutrition)

True Transformations begins with correcting the three keys cells:

The Keratinocytes
The Melanocytes
The Fibroblasts

Published studies have demonstrated that topically applied active ingredients can affect skin aging.

To have an effect the ingredient must:

- -Must be used by the patient
- –Penetrate surface layer of skin
- –Consistently deliver to specific layers of the skin
- –Induce a biological effect

Correction must start from the <u>inside</u> of the cell:

These are Rx drugs that make a cellular change.

–<u>Hydroquinone</u> is the most effective inhibitor of melanogenesis
It exerts its depigmenting effect by selective action on melanocyte metabolism. It lightens areas of darkened skin such as freckles, age spots, cholasma and melasma. Evidence of improvement is usually observed at 4-6 weeks. The improvement continues for about 4 months. It is proven safe and effective by FDA for 40+ years
2% Over-the-counter cosmetics
4% Prescription gold standard therapy for skin pigmentation disorders

–<u>Tretinoin</u> stimulates skin cell renewal by increasing the rate of mitotic cell division. It repairs DNA transcription by binding to nucleus receptors RAR and RXR. It corrects abnormal keratinocyte renewal while increasing fibroblast growth and collagen synthesis.

Influencing from the <u>outside</u> of a cell:

These are over the counter drugs.

–<u>Alpha Hydroxy Acids</u> mechanism of action is to exfoliate dead cells on the skin surface. They are replaced with more youthful cells (less dead) underneath, which are now closer to the surface. This creates superficial improvement and allows for improved penetration of active ingredients. It does not penetrate below the stratum corneum. Glycolic acid is the smaller molecule with the strongest exfoliation properties.
It is the most common type used in skin care products and chemical peels. Lactic acid is a large molecule and commonly found in moisturizers. It does not penetrate but sits on the surface.

–<u>Phytic Acid</u> acts as an exfoliate but is not an Alpha Hydroxy Acid. It is also a mild humectant due to its ability to exfoliate and expose less dehydrated keratinocytes. It is derived from plants and is a larger molecule then AHA's. This makes for less penetration and therefore less irritation.

–<u>Antioxidants (Vitamins C, E and A)</u> prepare the skin against exogenous oxidative stressors occurring daily. <u>Free radicals</u> form in the skin from UV-exposure causing DNA damage. The antioxidants have photo protective effects against the oxidative process helping to prevent future damage. The antioxidants are highly regarded in combating free radicals by neutralizing them. Antioxidants lend their own positive charge to the free radical before it can affect a healthy cell. Oxidation (premature damage) of the cell is, therefore, averted.

–<u>Hyaluronic Acid</u>   In the Dermis, the spaces between the fibers are filled with a composition of water, protein complexes and <u>hyaluronic acid.</u> It is a natural substance found in great abundance in young skin, and other tissues in humans and animals. This jelly-like complex is necessary for the transportation of essential nutrients from the bloodstream to the living cells of the skin. Oxygen radicals degrade and destroy hyaluronic acid over time. Fifty year olds are estimated to have less than half the hyaluronic acid they had in youth.

–<u>Sunscreens:</u>   Micronized Zinc Oxide – Z-Cote
is the preferred ingredient to combat skin aging
from UVA.
It protects against long UVA rays – up to 380
nm. It is recommended for daily use and on
compromised skin. Avobenzone provides UVA
protection in lesser wave lengths.
It is a chemical sunscreen for people with
concerns for irritation.

Octinoxate (formerly called Octyl
Methoxycinnamate)
Is a potent UVB absorber and chemical sunscreen
for–UVB 290-320 nm. It is currently the safest
UVB filter. It is widely used in sunscreen and
cosmetic preparations for daily wear.

We do have control over the rate at which our skin ages.

To slow and reverse skin aging requires a
comprehensive system approach. I think that the
consultation with a physician interested in skin
rejuvenation is well worth the time and money.

I have used the Obagi system personally and with my patients for over 10 years and have been amazed at the results obtained by nourishing and stimulating the skin to replace and renew the cells.

Pigmentation problems caused by the melanocytes also can be controlled once you understand the role and purpose for each cell type and the function it brings to skin health.

I much prefer the natural approach to nourishing the skin than the surgical approach applied by others.

Menopause.....

Today there is very confusing information about the treatment of menopause for the women of the world. Most women in America will tell you that hormones cause breast cancer. That is opinion.

The truth is that we do not know the cause of breast cancer. Some breast cancer seems to be affected, not caused by estrogen. This is breast cancer with positive estrogen receptors.

There is experience, out of America, that shows women given estrogen after breast cancer have less recurrences of their disease, and if it does come back, it grows less aggressively on estrogen.

I repeat that we do not understand breast cancer. When it occurs in woman under the age of menopause it seems to be much more aggressive than the breast cancer that occurs in woman who get their breast cancer after the age of menopause.

So what is a woman to do?

If it were not for breast cancer fear, most women would probably go on hormone replacement. The other risks are also theoretical more than actual. One of the problems is that the majority of hormone replacement in the last 50 years has been replacement of hormones foreign to the female body. We have used primarily horse or sweet potato hormones, which act like female hormones but are not female hormones. In addition they contain other hormones never found in human females.

Is it possible that the side effects are related to foreign hormones in women's bodies that were never intended to be there?

Just like our artificial food, we have been giving women artificial, foreign hormones. I contend that natural human hormones are safe. If they were not safe we should be removing women's ovaries early in life or at least when they complete their families, to keep women healthy. Why do women with the highest levels of hormones enjoy the prime of their life, if natural human hormones are bad?

We now have the ability give women hormones identical to what their ovaries made in the prime of their lives. We call these bio-identical hormones.

The ovary makes estrogens, progesterone, and testosterone. Women, with their natural hormones in their twenties, feel good hormonally. Things begin to change in the early thirties as the testosterone level begins to decrease with a subsequent decrease in the desire to be intimate with their partner. We call this a decreased libido, and lab tests confirm a level of testosterone often one third of the level that was present in their twenties.

It is in the middle thirties that the ovaries start making less progesterone, and we see an increase in premenstrual syndrome with mood swings and other symptoms. This is the beginning of peri-menopause (next to menopause).

In the late forties and early fifties the estrogen also drops. Irregular periods, hot flashes and eventually the end of periods and true menopause characterize this time of life.

Because of the fear of cancer, many women turn to herbal and nutritional solutions in order to treat their hormonal symptoms. Tang Kuei has been used by oriental women for centuries with evidence of success manifest by the lack of vocabulary words in the oriental languages for premenstrual syndrome and menopause. The intake of soy has also reduced the symptoms of irregular hormone release from the ovaries. There is much confusion over why soy works, however.

Soy actually seems to work as an anti-estrogen and works naturally like prescription medicines called SERMs. SERM stands for "Selective Estrogen Receptor Modulator" and actually competes for the estrogen receptor sites on women's tissues. The SERM prescription medications called Tamoxifen and Clomid and are used in treating breast cancer and infertility.

I again stress the fact that we really don't know all the answers. The human body is very complex. It is not simple. Anything we do affects many body systems. So every woman must decide for herself what she will do in regards to hormone replacement after the ovaries stop working.

We do know that hormones are protective in many ways. There is no question that the best prevention and treatment for osteoporosis is estrogen. Once again, osteoporosis is not as simple as that. Many lifestyle choices, however, enhance the development of osteoporosis. Drinking carbonated water (soda pop), lack of weight bearing activity (walking), lack of exposure to the sun (lower Vitamin D), diets low in calcium, smoking of tobacco and drinking of alcohol, all increase the development of thinning of the bones. The early stages are called osteopenia.

The theories and facts on hormone replacement are obscure. Once again the decision and responsibility for the results must be made by the woman herself and not her doctor. However, if hormones were to be used, I would make a plea that you take bio-identical hormones, which must be prepared by a compounding pharmacy. With your doctor and pharmacist, you can create a designer hormone blend that is made specifically for you and your body. It is then important that you carefully track your symptoms and how you feel so that the dose can be adjusted until you feel hormonally at 60 like you did hormonally at 20. That is possible and can be done.

So, to take hormones or not take hormones, that is the question. I would suggest we again refer back to our ancient DNA. Did that woman 40,000 years ago have the same symptoms that the woman of today experiences? We do not know. Her activities, her food, her life was nothing like the life we lead today. She probably had periods start later in life. She may have only had two or three periods her entire life. She got pregnant as soon as she was fertile. She nursed all her children and then got pregnant again while nursing as soon as she ovulated. Menopause came earlier in life. Thousands of years of artificial nutrition have changed women's bodies. We, therefore, must make our decision based on what we know today.

The area that remains the most confusing to me regards the mental performance of women as they age. There is evidence that there is <u>less</u> senile dementia and Alzheimers in women who use hormone replacement for life. There are also studies showing <u>more</u> mental impairment in women using hormones.

All I know is that thousands of woman have told me in peri-menopause, when hormones are beginning to decline, that they experience forgetfulness, depression, irritability, difficulty concentrating, and "brain fog". When placed on hormone replacement this almost universally improves.

If I were a woman, I would take bio-identical hormones for life. That is what my female family members are doing.

Exercise May Be Dangerous to Your Health..........

Wow! Is that possible?

It is not only possible but, in my opinion, true! That is certainly a provocative statement.

We are continually feeling guilty that we are not exercising enough. How many exercise infomercials do you see every night on late TV? We have an obsession with our weight and have been told that exercise holds the key to losing what we don't want. Is it possible to lose by not exercising? I actually find it easier to get a person in a wheel chair to lose weight than a "gymaholic".

I can make sure the wheel chair person takes in adequate calories and does not get tempted to exercise beyond their caloric intake. When the gym person starts to lose they begin to feel better and logically deduce that more exercise will make it happen sooner. This just creates more starvation instead of nutrition unless they increase their calories. They usually refuse to do that and the vicious malnutrition cycle is maintained while they get their high off of endorphins artificially as their body tries to keep them alive.

Let us return to our ancient ancestors' lifestyle of survival of the fittest and the smartest. Every time we ventured from our home it was a life threatening experience. We might not return from the hunt due to injury from a wild animal. An enemy tribe might capture us. They might steal our family while we were gone. We might have encountered storms or natural disasters. Home was safe and the outside world was dangerous.

When home, we spent time holding our children, recounting stories of the family, and having mental and physical contact with the ones we loved. This was primitive life at its best. So where was the exercise?

Perhaps that one-minute sprint from the charging buffalo was "exercise"? How about carrying our kill home? Racing back home was exercise when we heard the screams of our family as roving enemy hunting parties molested them. Maybe throwing boulders at attacking enemies was exercise.

Are you getting the picture? You see the ancients who tried to outrun the buffalo or saber tooth tiger, were killed and their genes taken out of the gene pool. Those ancients smart enough to hide or climb a tree quickly, lived. Those who tried to use their muscle rather than their brain died. Hence our DNA is from the thinkers, not the runners!

We did not begin hard physical work until 10,000 years ago when we began an agricultural life style. That is also when the modern plague of heart disease, cancer, high blood pressure and stroke and diabetes began. Agriculture allowed civilization to evolve. We now developed concentrations of people in cities who were no longer dependant on hunting and gathering or nomadic herding of flocks of domesticated animals.

I, therefore, feel that the physiologic exercise compatible with our DNA is probably

- Walking
- Sprinting for a minute and climbing a tree
- Throwing boulders
- Carrying home loads on our shoulders
- Dragging heavy things
- Carrying our children
- Swimming against currents
- Hopping from boulder to boulder
- Leaping across ravines
- Throwing a spear

Most of these require short bursts of focused

power called high-intensity work. This kind of fitness, generating short bursts of maximum power, involves an anaerobic (without oxygen) type of energy production. Our early ancestors were also aerobically fit, but this came from walking, not running. There are stories of the American Indian who would sometimes track an animal for several days during times of famine, but this was not a frequent occurrence.

Mankind, just liked wild animals, was born to be fit, not fat. It is lack of nutrition not lack of exercise that has made us fat. Our ancient ancestors became very efficient in hunting and gathering to limit the time they were away from the safety of home.

Remember that we had physical activity characterized by bursts of high intensity activity lasting only a few minutes followed by long periods of relaxing, storytelling, stretching and napping.

Overtraining, ie. repetitively performing too much of the same sort of exercise, can actually damage your health and happiness, impair your performance, increase your risk for severe injury, and leave you more susceptible to infections and possibly even cancers.

You want to do the whole body exercise that your DNA was intended to do. Remember that wellness is your birthright. In the world of power exercise, more is not better. There is just the right amount. It also takes 48 hours to repair the muscle injured by high intensity exercise.

The perfect DNA exercise in my opinion if you want a machine, is the ROM, which stands for "Range of Motion". These are made in California with the research to confirm the O_2 burned in the muscle done at University of Southern California in the 90s. Information on the ROM can be obtained from the manufacturer in Appendix VIII.

Remember the morning started with stretching for our ancestors as they greeted the sun as it rose in the East. Night was again ended with stretching as they laid down for the night's rest.

If you have ever heard the cry at the gym "No Pain, No Gain" I would beg you to forget this self defeating, health destroying philosophy. Self inflicted pain is NOT NATURAL! Physical activity does not have to hurt to help. Pain is to be avoided. You would think anyone was crazy who was hurting themselves doing anything except exercise. It is another lie perpetuated by ignorant experts.

More is not always better, and this is absolutely true for exercise. Moderate exercise relieves stress, but over exercising --- too much or too often--- adds stress, raises cortisol (the bodies stress hormone) and it increases insulin levels. Moderate exercise strengthens the immune defenses, but with over exercise immunity is decreased. Exercise scientists can record a measurable fall in levels of white blood cells, which fight disease, after overly vigorous exercise. The white blood cell count does not return to normal for 24-48 hours. If you beat yourself up day after day you will decrease your immune defenses and be more prone to colds, sore throats and nagging injuries. The decrease in immune defense also increases your chance of developing cancer.

Now lastly, lets look at our children. I repeatedly hear "experts" bemoan the obesity epidemic of our children caused by lack of physical activity. After all, everyone knows that our kids are fat from sitting in front of TV and computer screens instead of riding their bikes and playing outside. This is another LIE!!!! Lack of nutrition, not lack of exercise has made our children fat. We feed them unphysiologic breakfasts of grain and refined sugar and feed them nothing close to the diet their DNA needs.

How much exercise did our ancient ancestor's children get?

NOT MUCH IF THEY WERE TO SURVIVE TO ADULTHOOD!!!!

Think about it! They died if they left home. They were weak, slow, and fragile. They stayed with the women at home until they became men and then went on the hunts or they gathered with the women. Young girls learned to prepare clothing and food and stayed home. Where was the physical activity? Why weren't they fat? They were fit because they ate the food they were supposed to eat for their DNA.

Our children can be as fit using their brains not their brawn! It's their birthright!

Is Alternative Medicine an Alternative?..

We are surrounded by medical care choices today. Never have there been so many and in such a confusing format. Each seems to claim to be the absolute solution to almost every ailment known to human kind.

293

Each form of care has its loyal followers, which seem to almost be deciples of a cult. Who are you to believe?

If you try to discuss them with your "Primary Care Physician" you will be scoffed at at best and ridiculed at worst! Why bother to tell them what you are experimenting with? They will think you are silly or even worse....... stupid.

What is one to do? Testimonials abound for "secret" cures from some obscure corner of the earth.

I have had an open mind since I was a child. My mother was a practitioner of "pioneer" cures and Vermont folk medicine. I took lots of vinegar and honey growing up and never saw a doctor. "Vicks" mentholatum and ice and heat were used regularly. "Feed a Fever and Starve a Cold" were mantras my mother would sing out as she stirred concoctions on the stove that encouraged you to get better just by their noxious smells.

As a Boy Scout, I learned first aid, and that helped me during my medical school rotations in the emergency room more than classroom lectures.

I grew up thinking only people who were dying went to see doctors. The only time I would see our neighbor, Dr. James Stout, was when I needed a physical for Boy Scout Camp. I never missed school or work due to sickness. Mom's cures were worse than school!

This was the background I brought to medical school. My first day in my life to visit a hospital was my first day in medical school!

When I learned about Navajo Sings and Hispanic Folk Healers, I was a believer. When I saw the "laying on of hands" and prayer at church to heal the sick "in the household of faith", I believed. How could I do anything else. I saw people cured.

As a missionary doctor in Nepal, I saw mysterious healings by holy men and folk healers that were astonishing. I accepted that there were many ways to heal and comfort besides with a scalpel or prescription pad.

I do not know anything about the myriad of health alternatives available today. I hear of new ones all the time. Are they quacks or charlatans? I honestly don't know.

My suggestion is that you ask for content

patients and interview them before signing for an expensive new treatment. Be responsible for making your own decision for treatment. Don't get talked into anything.

Ayurveda
Reconnective Therapy
Homeopathy
Naturopaths
Napropaths
Jin Shin Jyitsu
Toggling (Cognitive Polar Transformation)
Bach Flower Therapy
Chiropractic
Therapeutic Massage
Reiki
Hellerwork
Polarity Therapy
Cranial Sacral Therapy
Shamanism
Therapeutic Breathing
Healing Hands
Acupressure
Acupuncture
Phrenology

The list is not even a fraction of what is available.

Just like the stories of wonder parts for cars that

make them get 100 miles to the gallon and are bought up by the oil companies, there are similar stories of pharmaceutical companies and doctors suppressing new therapies that compete with their cures and livelihood. I do not know whether this is true or not. I would hope not.

I would again caution as well as encourage your open mind to the aids available to the physiology of your body.

With many alternative therapies people get better, but who really knows if it was the cure or applied treatment or just the wonderful body curing itself?

Give the body a chance to straighten out with the right rest and nutrition and miracles are sure to happen.

Sometimes the vinegar and honey may be the best cure with a tincture of time!

The Final Word.........

Quality of life as well as quantity should be our goal.

Remember:

YOU WERE BORN TO BE HEALTHY AND THIN!

One of my best friends, Dr. Jamie McManus, has given the best definition for wellness I have ever heard.

"Wellness is being able to get up in the morning and do whatever you want."

Not being limited by mind or body is a wonderful blessing.

You were born to be healthy.

You were born to be thin.

I hope this owner's manual to your body will help you to have and live a great and healthy life.

If I were to summarize the key points of this book, what would they be? What can anyone do?

1. Breathing may kill you.
2. Talents come from hard work. They are not natural.
3. You were born to learn anything and you can.

4. Like yourself!
5. Keep everything in balance
6. Keep it natural.
7. Learn to listen to your body! Get to know its feelings. Get in rhythm and harmony with your physiology.
8. Realize that you, as a human, are different than the other living things on the earth, and find your destiny.
9. Meditate daily.
10. Shun grains except as a survival food.
11. Eat healthy fats from olive oil and fish.
12. Supplement for the lost nutrition in our food.
13. Control your Insulin.
14. Remember to have a colorful diet of fruits and vegetables.
15. Be teachable.
16. Appreciate your skin.
17. The sun is not your friend.
18. Meat is good.
19. Cholesterol may not be bad.
20. Less Omega 6 (grain) and more Omega 3 (fish oil)
21. Believe you have control of your health.
22. Find new interests in life and be a lifetime learner.
23. Eat what you were naturally made to eat.

24. Engage in intense, short duration exercise daily.
25. Use every minute of the day. You will eventually run out of tomorrows.
26. Live your life for you, not anyone else!

2400 years ago,

HIPPOCRATES
the
"Father of Modern Medicine"
said ....

"let food be your medicine and let medicine be your food."

Today, there is overwhelming scientific evidence to suggest that Hippocrates was right!

Add physical activity, supplements, peace of mind, and you might find man once again living for hundreds, if not thousands of years.

Sing Life's Song at the Top of Your Lungs!

You are Unique.

You are Special.

Life is Divine.

Nutrition = Life

And in the words of that Intergalactic Jedi Philosopher......
Yoda

"Try Not....
Do or Do Not....
There is No Try!"

May Life's **FORCE**
Be With YOU!

Appendix I.

Books Worth Reading
For the Details

These were the books I found most helpful in
my quest for more light and knowledge about
how my body was meant to function and what
I needed to know as its owner. Not all of them
agree with what I have presented in this book as
my opinions today.

All of them made me think, question, ponder and
decide. I hope my book will do the same for you.

Allan, Christine *Life Without Bread* Los Angeles: Keats Publishing,
(2000)

Arnot, Bob *The Breast Cancer Protection Plan* Boston: Little,
Brown and Company, (1998)

Arnot, Bob *The Prostate Cancer Protection Plan* Boston: Little,
Brown and Company, (2000)

Audette, Ray *Neander Thin* New York: St. Martin's Press, (1999)

Bernstein, Richard *Dr. Bernstein's Diabetes Solution* Boston: Little
and Brown and Company, (1997)

Blaylock, Russell *Excitotoxins: the Taste That Kills* New York:
Health Press, (1996)

Braly, James *Dangerous Grains* New York: Avery, (2002)

Burns, Stephanie *Great Lies We Live By* Australia: Navybridge Pty Limited, (2004)

Challem, Jack *The Inflammation Syndrome* New Jersey: John Wiley & sons, Inc., (2003)
Coats, Bill *Aloe Vera: The New Millennium* New York: iUniverse, Inc., (2003)

Cordain, Loren *The Paleo Diet* New York: John Wiley and Sons, Inc., (2002)

Deron, Scott *C-reactive Protein* New York: Contemporary Books, (2004)

Eades, Michael and Mary Dan *Protein Power* New York: Warner Books, (1996)

Eades, Michael and Mary Dan *The Protein Power Lifeplan* New York: Warner Books, (2000)

Eckstein, Gustav *The Body Has A Head* New York: Harper Row Publishers, (1970)

Heber, David *What Color Is Your Diet* New York: Harper Collins Books, (2001)

Heber, David *The L.A. Shape Diet* New York: Harper Collins Books, (2004)

Hill, Napoleon *Think and Grow Rich* New York: Hawthorn Books Inc., (1937)

Ignarro, Louis *NO More Heart Disease* New York: St. Martin's Press, (2005)

Kahn, Robert *Successful Aging* New York: Delacorte Press, (1999)

McManus, Jamie *Your Personal Guide to Wellness* United States of America: New Horizons Communications, (2004)

Meggs, William *The Inflammation Cure* New York: Contemporary Books, (2004)

Mercola, Joseph *The No-Grain Diet* New York: Dutton, (2003)

Miller, Dave *Herbal Products Reference Guide 16th edition* Salt Lake City: Wholistic Health Publishers, (2005)

Perls, Thomas *Living to 100* New York: Basic Books, (2000)

Pilzer, Paul Zane *The Wellness Revolution* New York: John Wiley & Sons, Inc. (2002)

Reiss, Uzzi *Natural Hormone Balance For Women* New York: Pocket Books Health, (2001)

Rohn, Jim *The Five Major Pieces to the Life Puzzle* Dallas: Great Impressions Printing and Graphics, (1991)

Sears, Barry *The Anti Inflammation Zone* New York: Reagan Books, (2005)

Sears, Barry *The Zone* New York: Reagan Books, (1995)

Sears, Barry *The Anti-Aging Zone* New York: Reagan Books, (1999)

Sears, Barry *The Omega Rx Zone* New York: Reagan Books, (2002)

Sears, Barry *The Top 100 Zone Foods* New York: Reagan Books, (2001)

Sears, Barry *What to Eat in The Zone* New York: Reagan Books, (2001)

Schwarzbein, Diana *The Schwarzbein Principle II* Florida: Health Communications, Inc., (2002)

Sitchin, Zecharia *The Earth Chronicles* New York: Avon Books, (1980)

Simontacchi, Carol *The Crazy Makers* New York: Putnam, (2000)

Smith, Melissa *Going Against The Grain* Chicago: Contemporary Books, (2002)

Snowdon, David *Aging With Grace* New York: Bantam Books, (2001)

Somer, Elizabeth *The Orgin Diet* New York: Henry Holt and Company, (2001)

Stoff, Jesse *The Prostate Miracle* New York: Kennsington Books, (2000)

Summers, Suzanne *The Sexy Years* New York: Random House, (2004)

Vanderhaeghe, Lorna and Karst, Karlene *Healthy Fats For Life* Canada: Quarry Health, (2003)

Vendryes, Anthony *An Ounce of Prevention* Jamaica: Tony Vendryes Enterprises Limited, (2002)

Vliet, Elizabeth Lee *It's My Ovaries, Stupid* New York: Scribner, (2003)

Vliet, Elizabeth Lee *Screaming To Be Heard* New York: M. Evans and C0ompany, Inc., (1995)

Appendix II.

Glycemic Load Explained

In the not too distant past, it was believed that foods containing sugar were "bad" because they caused blood sugar levels to rapidly escalate, whereas carbohydrates were "good" because their effect was more delayed.

Recently it's been discovered that some foods release their sugar slowly, and other carbohydrate-containing foods have a "flash" fast effect on blood sugar levels.

Researchers began testing how quickly specific foods like beets and oatmeal convert to glucose (blood sugar), comparing them to white table sugar or white bread. They set a standard measure – how quickly will 50 grams of the particular food's carbohydrates turn to sugar. That's called Glycemic Index (GI).

What Glycemic Index (GI) *doesn't* tell us is how many carbohydrates are in a serving. This presents a problem. For example, you might think a cola soda pop, with a GI of 90 is better than cranberry juice because it has a GI of 105 (compared to white bread). You might be tempted to eliminate carrots from your diet due their

extremely high GI value (131, using white bread as the base).

Common sense tells you that a berry-based drink should be better than a sugar-based soda pop or that carrots have got to be good for you. That's where Glycemic Load (GL) comes in: it takes into consideration a food's Glycemic Index as well as the amount of carbohydrates per serving.

A carrot has only four grams of carbohydrate. To get 50

grams, you'd have to eat about a pound and a half of them! GL takes the GI value and multiplies it by the actual number of carbohydrates in a serving.

Carrots 131% x 4 =

5 Glycemic Load

By contrast, a cup of cooked pasta has a GI of 71 and a whopping 40 grams of carbohydrates giving it a GL of 28.

Cup of Pasta 71% x 40 =

28 Glycemic Load

What Determines GI and GL?

Since the values are based on carbohydrates, the values to a large degree are determined by how many grams there are per serving, and how quickly the carbohydrate is broken down into glucose. Several factors come into play:

- Amount of cooking: Starches in food swell when cooked (whether it's boiled, broiled, baked, or fried). The starch grains in a baked potato swell to the bursting point, whereas the starch grains in brown rice remain relatively unchanged.

- Amount of processing: When grains are rolled, ground, or smashed, the protective (and harder to digest) outer coating is removed. Whole oats have a lower GI than oatmeal, which is made from smashed oat grains.

- Amount of fiber: Some foods naturally have higher amounts of fiber – for example beans and legumes. Unprocessed foods (for example brown rice) have greater amounts of fiber than processed foods (white rice).

- Amount of fat: The more fat there is in a food, the longer it takes to digest. GL values are interesting – and somewhat useful. But they're available on a limited basis, and don't take into account any valuable vitamins and minerals found in a particular food. To be healthy, get sufficient nutrients and fiber, and avoid a blood sugar "spike":

- Choose a wide variety of non-starchy vegetables

- Eat fruits and starchy vegetables with high protein or high fiber foods

- Use healthy fats – nuts, seeds, fish, and mono unsaturated oils (olive, soybean, et cetera)

- Lose weight (if you're overweight)

The best tables for Glycemic Index compared to Glycemic Load are from the Sydney University Glycemic Index Research Service. They may be accessed on line at

<u>http://www.ajcn.org/cgi/reprint/76/1/5.pdf</u>

or by searching for the Sydney University Glycemic Index Research Service with any search engine.   The tables are 63 pages long and not reproduced here.

<u>Glycemic Load</u>
1-10 good
10-20 moderate
20-? Bad

Glycemic Index vs. Glycemic Load

Food

	GI	GL
Bananas	52	12
Grapes	46	8
Orange	42	5
Peach	42	5
Pear	38	5
Raisins	64	28
Strawberry	40	1
Watermelon	72	4
Apple	38	6
Jelly Bean	78	22
Peanut	14	1
French Fries	75	22
Sweet Potato	61	17
Baked Potato	85	26
Boiled Potato	101	17
Corn	54	9
Green Pea	48	3
Pumpkin	75	3

Appendix III.

HIGH PROTEIN FOODS

The average protein content of foods below is listed in grams in parentheses next to the name of the food.

- ## MEATS & MEAT SUBSTITUTES:

    o 3 ounces cooked fresh water fish (21)

    o 1/2 cup canned tuna (14)

    o 3 ounces cooked shellfish (19)

    o 3 ounces cooked chicken, turkey, or other poultry (24)

    o 3 ounces cooked beef, pork, lamb or other red meat (21)

    o 1 large egg (6)

    o 1/4 cup fat-free egg substitute (5)

    o 1/2 cup roasted soybeans (34)

    o 1/2 cup tofu or tempeh (10)

    o 1 cup soy milk (4)

    o 1 cup cooked dried beans, like pinto, kidney, or navy (15)

    o 1 cup cooked dried peas or lentils (17)

- **DAIRY:**

  - o 1 cup any type of fresh milk (8)

  - o 1 cup buttermilk (8)

  - o 1/2 cup evaporated canned milk (9)

  - o 1/4 cup nonfat dry milk (11)

  - o 1 ounce semi-hard or solid cheese (7)

  - o 1/4 cup parmesan cheese (8)

  - o 1/2 cup cottage cheese (14)

  - o 1/2 cup custard (7)

  - o 1/2 cup pudding (4)

  - o 8 ounces plain or fruit yogurt (8)

- **NUTS & SEEDS:**
  (also lots of fat and calories)

  - o 2 Tbsp almonds, cashews, or walnuts (5)

  - o 2 Tbsp peanut butter (8)

  - o 2 Tbsp peanuts (7)

  - o 2 Tbsp sesame tahini (5)

  - o 2 Tbsp sunflower nuts (5)

Appendix IV.

DR. KOMADINA'S
FOOD EXCHANGES

Fruit:
Fruits contain 15 grams of carbohydrate and 60 calories.
One exchange equals:
1 small apple, banana, orange, nectarine
1 medium fresh peach
2 small plums, apricots
½ banana
1 kiwi
1/2 grapefruit
1/2 mango
1 cup fresh berries (strawberries, raspberries or blueberries)
1 cup fresh cantaloupe or watermelon cubes
1/8th honeydew
4 ounces unsweetened juice
½ cup diced pineapple

DAIRY:
There are three milk exchange lists:
1. Fat-free, low-fat milk choices
2. Reduced-fat milk choices
3. Whole milk choices

Fat-Free and Very Low-Fat Milk
Fat-free and very lowfat milk contain 12 grams
carbohydrates, 8 grams protein, 0-3
grams fat, and 90 calories per serving.
One exchange equals:
1 cup milk, fat-free or 1% fat
3/4 cup yogurt, plain non fat or low fat
1 cup yogurt, artificially sweetened

Reduced-Fat Milk

Reduced-fat milk choices have 12 grams carbohydrates, 8 grams protein, 5 grams
fat, and 120 calories per serving.
One serving equals:
1 cup milk, 2%
1 cup milk, soy
3/4 cup yogurt, plain and low-fat

Whole Milk

Whole milk choices have 12 grams carbohydrates, 8 grams protein, 8 grams fat, and 150 calories per serving.
One serving equals:
1 cup milk, whole
1/2 cup evaporated whole milk
3/4 cup yogurt, plain from whole milk
1 cup kefir

NON-STARCHY VEGETABLES:

Vegetables contain 25 calories, 2 grams protein, and 5 grams
of carbohydrate.
One exchange equals:

1/2 cup cooked vegetables (carrots, broccoli, zucchini, cabbage, green beans,
squash, mushrooms, sprouts, spinach, beets, eggplant, greens, brussel sprouts,
cauliflower)
1 cup raw vegetables or salad greens
1/2 cup vegetable juice
1 large tomato
½ cucumber
2 stalks of celery
½ bell pepper
1/2 onion
 9 spears of asparagus

Starch:

Starches contain 15 grams of carbohydrate, 3 grams protein, 0-1 grams fat, and 80
calories per serving.
One exchange equals:
1 slice bread (white, pumpernickel, whole wheat, rye)
2 slice reduced calorie or "lite" bread
1/4 (1 ounce) bagel (varies)
1/2 English muffin
1/2 hamburger bun
3/4 cup cold cereal
1/3 cup rice, brown or white- cooked
1/3 cup barley or couscous- cooked
1/3 cup legumes (dried beans, peas or lentils), cooked
1/2 cup pasta- cooked
1/2 cup bulgar- cooked
1/2 cup corn, sweet potato or green peas
3 ounce baked sweet or white potato
3/4 ounce pretzels
3 cups popcorn, hot air popped or microwave (80% light)

LEAN PROTEIN:

Lean protein choices have 55 calories, 7 grams protein, and 3 grams of fat per
serving.
One exchange equals:
1 ounce chicken- dark meat, skin removed
1 ounce turkey- dark meat, skin removed
1 ounce salmon, Swordfish, herring
1 ounce lean beef (flank steak, London broil,
    tenderloin, roast beef)*
1 ounce veal, roast or lean chop*
1 ounce lamb, roast or lean chop*
1 ounce pork, tenderloin or fresh ham*
1 ounce low fat cheese (3 grams or less of fat per ounce)
1 ounce low fat luncheon meats (3 gms or less of fat/ ounce)

1/4 cup 4.5% cottage cheese
2 medium sardines
• Limit to 1-2 times per week

MEDIUM-FAT PROTEIN:
Medium fat protein choices have 75 calories, 7 grams protein, and 5 grams of fat per
serving.
One exchange equals:
1 ounce beef (any prime cut), corned beef, ground beef **
1 ounce pork chop
1 each whole egg (medium) **
1 ounce mozzarella cheese
1/4 cup ricotta cheese
4 ounces tofu (note this is a Heart Healthy choice)
** choose these very infrequently

HIGH-FAT PROTEIN:
High fat meat choices are high in saturated fat and cholesterol, and should be eaten
in moderation. High fat protein choices have 100 calories,
7 grams protein, and 8 grams of fat per serving.
One exchange equals:
1 oz. regular cheese (e.g., American, Swiss, cheddar)
1 oz. Polish sausage
1 tablespoon peanut butter
1 oz. Spareribs

FAT:
Fats contain 45 calories and 5 grams of fat per serving.
One exchange equals:
1 teaspoon oil (vegetable, corn, canola, olive, etc.)
1 teaspoon butter
1 teaspoon mayonnaise
1 Tablespoon reduced fat mayonnaise
1 Tablespoon salad dressing
1 Tablespoon cream cheese
2 Tablespoons lite cream cheese
1/8th avocado
8 large black olives
10 large stuffed green olives
1 slice bacon

Appendix V.

Dr. Komadina's Ten Commandments of <u>DNA</u> Food Choices

Thou Shall Eat:

1. Fish, Fowl and Meat
2. Berries and Fruits
3. Vegetables
4. Greens
5. Nuts and Seeds

Thou Shall Not Eat:

6. Grains
7. Beans
8. Potatoes
9. Dairy
10. Sugar

If you can't get it with a pointed stick or eat it raw, then your DNA may not have been designed for you to eat it at all.

Thou Shall Eat

Meat and Fish

beef, veal, lamb, pork, venison, chicken, turkey, duck, pheasant, quail, rabbit, buffalo, moose, elk, seal, bear, squid, octopus, goose, oysters, clams, mussels, lobster, crayfish, halibut, cod, salmon, eel, trout, bass, carp, sardines, tuna, whitefish, orange roughie, sole, and any other forms of meat or meat byproducts and organs including lard.

Fruits

apples, cherries, pears, peaches, melons, cucumbers, tomatoes, bananas, avocados, plums, olives, figs, dates, mangoes, kiwi, star fruit, pineapple, pomegranates, passion fruit, peppers, watermelon, cantaloupe, honeydew melon, oranges, lemons, limes, tangerines, tangelos, citrons, nectarines, papaya or any other fruit eaten fresh if possible

Vegetables and Greens
lettuce, cabbage, kohlrabi, kale, rhubarb,
cauliflower, flowers, broccoli, asparagus,
parsley, spinach, celery, carrots, onions,
mushrooms, greens, radish, leek, endive,
dandelion, brussel sprouts, artichoke, mint,
basil, marjoram, oregano, rosemary, sage,
thyme, fennel, garlic, shallots, bay leaves,
cloves, saffron and any other part of
the plant that is edible raw

Nuts and Seeds
almonds, walnuts, pecans, brazil nuts, acorns,
hickory, filberts, macadamia, flax, sesame,
poppy, coriander, celery, anise, caraway,
chervil, cumin, dill, fennel, mustard, and
any other that are edible raw

Berries
grapes, blueberries, raspberries,
blackberries, boysenberries, strawberries,
currants, and any other edible raw

Thou Shall Not Eat

Grains
Corn, wheat, barley, rye, rice, oats, millet, and all products made from them

Beans
Including all varieties of hard beans, lima beans, pinto beans, kidney beans, green beans, wax beans, peas, peanuts, chocolate, fava, and all products made from them

Potatoes
All variety of potatoes and yams, beets, taro, cassava (tapioca), turnips, and all products made from them

Dairy
Milk, cheese, yogurt, butter, and all products made from them

Sugar
Fructose, sucrose, maltose, dextrose, lactose, corn sweeteners, molasses, and all products made from them

Appendix VI

Body Composition Science

A comparison of methods for assessing human body composition.

Height/Weight Tables

In 1953 the Metropolitan Life Insurance Company developed the first height/weight tables to calculate the degree of individuals over or under weight status. The data was based on "averages" from its client base for both men and women. In 1983 the tables were revised based on updated data.

Frame size is an important, subjective factor utilized in the development of the tables with small, medium and large frame determinations changing the "ideal weight" recommendation. Improvement on frame size determinations were implemented in 1986 with the elbow breadth or wrist circumference measurements used to classify frame size.

The use of the Metropolitan height/weight table gives no indication as to the degree of either obesity or leanness on an individual basis. In the individual clinical setting, height/weight tables can provide grossly inaccurate conclusions about an individual's health risk. The validity of estimation of percent body fat and density by height and weight measurements when compared to the Hydrostatic tank is very poor with correlation coefficients in range of .31 to .43.

Body Mass Index (BMI)

Body Mass Index has recently been used to quantify an individual's obesity level. BMI is derived from a ratio equation of height squared divided by weight. Here again, only an individual's height and weight are used and no indication of actual lean or fat mass can be determined. Thus, BMI offers little advantage over the existing Metropolitan tables.

Skin Fold Measurements

The test methodology for body fat estimation with skin fold measurements requires the use of a "caliper device" to measure the thickness of substantial fat stores. The assumption is that substantial fat is proportional to over all body fat and thus by measuring several sites total body fat may be calculated.

There are many site measurements where skin fold measurements can be taken. Currently over 100 different equations are available to estimate body fat with the use of skin fold calipers. The wide variety of equations reflects the problem with the accuracy of this methodology.

There are many limitations with the Skin Fold measurement technique. The validity of skin fold measurements is at best ±6% compared to the hydrostatic tank. Because of the inaccuracy associated with skin fold calipers, many credible organizations such as the U.S. Army and the Los Angeles Police Department have abandoned the use of them.

Inter-operator Error

The estimation results obtained from skin fold measurements vary widely from technician to technician. The "art" of skin fold measurements requires the technician to properly identify a site measurement and pinch the skin gathering only the fat store and no other tissue. The error of estimate between technicians has been reported to be ±8%.

Fat Storage

The assumption that 50% of human body fat is located in subcutaneal tissues and the remaining 50% is found in intra-muscular and essential fat (around organs) is not universally valid. Body fat distribution and health risk varies depending on genetics, exercise and nutritional patterns.

Fat Thickness and Density

The obese population represents unique limitations for skin fold measurements. Skin fold calipers cannot open wide enough to measure the total fat thickness, thus tends to grossly under estimate body fat percentage in the obese population. Also of concern, especially in the obese population, is the compression of fat by the caliper due to variances in fat density. Again, this tends to inaccurately estimate percent fat in the obese, the population where accuracy is most important.

Near Infrared Interactance

The use of Infrared (IR) light to measure fat is not a new technique. The U.S.D.A first developed the technique to measure the fat contained in 1 cubic centimeter sections of beef and pork carcasses after slaughter. In the human device, a "wand" from the device emits an IR light source at about 900 nanometers into the biceps area. The methodology is based on the ability of fat tissues to "absorb" more IR light than lean tissue, which can then be measured as a change in the infrared level.

The only commercially available unit to predict human body composition is manufactured by Futrex. Since the Futrex device was first marketed for clinical use, many research articles have been published stating that the device is not accurate and is not recommended for clinical use in the assessment of body composition. The original application of this IR technology was developed on "skinned" carcasses. No research is available about IR penetration through the skin.

The actual contribution of the IR wand measurement and input into the height and weight calculations used in the device's program has also been questioned. This device has not been approved by the FDA for this use.

Hydrostatic Weighing

Hydrostatic Weighing is currently considered the "Gold Standard" of body composition analysis. Hydrostatic measurements are based on the assumption hat density and specific gravity of lean tissue is greater than that of fat tissue. Lean tissue will sink in water and fat tissue will float. By comparing a test subject's mass measured under water and out of the water, body composition may be calculated. The "Gold Standard" of body composition is a mathematical prediction.

Bioelectrical Impedance

The use of bioelectrical impedance was first documented in 1880 (Kalvin), as a potentially safe, convenient and accurate technique to measure conductivity in the body.

The method is based on the fact that the lean tissue of the body is much more conductive due to its higher water content than fat tissue. A bioimpedance meter is attached to the body, at the extremities, and a small 500-800 micro-amp, 50 kilohertz, signal measures the body's ability to conduct the current. The more lean tissue present in the body the greater the conductive potential, measured in ohms.

Linear Regression Formulas

In the early 1980's, the first commercial bioimpedance units were available to measure human body composition (RJL, Valhalla, Space Labs etc.). These bioimpedance units utilize "linear regression" formulas to predict body fat based on biological data input into a single equation.

A review of the literature indicates that bioimpedance units which utilize these linear regression equations tend to be somewhat valid for a "normal" population, but under-predict body fat for obese subjects and over-predict body fat of lean subjects. The standard errors of estimate for these equations are ±5% to ±6.4% in normal populations when compared to the hydrostatic tank.

ElectroLipoGraphy (ELG)

In 1985, the first validated algorithmic equations to interpret bioimpedance measurements were developed and patented by BIO/ANALOGICS. The use of the algorithmic equations instead of linear regression allows for population specific variables for lean, obese, elderly and pediatric subjects.

The National Institutes of Health (NIH) conference on bio-impedance analysis (1994) concluded that to obtain valid predictions of percent body fat in humans, population specific equations must be applied.

The algorithmic equations developed and patented by BiO/ANALOGICS are population specific and validated on all types of subjects. The current validation studies contain more than 1000 subjects with an error factor of ±3.3% and a correlation coefficient of .88 compared to the criterion hydrostatic tank.

As mentioned earlier, the accepted test/re-test variance with hydrostatic measurements is 2.5% when compared to itself. The accepted test/re-test variance for bioimpedance analysis is less than ±.5%.

Anthro-ElectroLipoGraphy (ELGII)

Anthro-ElectroLipoGraphy, the new, state of the art technology, utilizes the algorithmic approach of ElectroLipoGraphy (ELG) coupled with specific anthropometric measurements to further define body fat measurements. This technique was developed by BIO/ANALOGICS to further improve the original, patented algorithmic formula.

A total of five (5) to six (6) site measurements are entered into the algorithmic formula to increase the correlation coefficient to .91, and to reduce the standard error of estimate to ±2.8% compared to the hydrostatic tank. No other clinically available unit provides the Scientific accuracy, reliability and efficiency across a wide range of subjects.

Appendix VII.
Essential Fats

Omega – 6
(From Grain)

Cause the blood to be more prone to clot
Promote rapid growth of cells
Induce smooth muscles cells to contract
Bring about an inflammatory response
Causes pain.

Omega – 3
(from Fish Oil)

Blood Thinner
Slows the growth of cells
Relaxes smooth muscle contractions
Anti inflammatory response
Relieves Pain
Repairs the brain
Repairs nerve sheaths

Appendix VIII

Recommended Sources of items mentioned in this book

Pharmaceutical Grade Fish Oil:
    Health Horizons
    505-893-2840

Body Composition Testing Equipment:
    USA ProHealth, Inc.
    http:www.usaprohealth.com
    1-800-230-9052

Range of Motion Exercise Machines:
    QuickGymNM
    505-269-7349
    http://www.quickgymnm.com

Training to Become a Nutrition Coach:
    Steven Komadina, M.D.
    505-893-2840

Information on joining Dr. Komadina in his Nutrition – Health Mission: 505-893-2840

Weight Loss Coaching From Dr. Komadina's Team: 505-893-2840

Author

NEW MEXICO STATE SENATOR
STEVEN A. KOMADINA, M.D.,
F.A.C.O.G.

Doctor, Senator, Grandpa, Dad, Hubby all apply to Steve Komadina. You will get to know him, as he candidly unveils his thoughts on the wonderful bodies we live with daily.

Humorous, frightening, irreverent, and courageous are all descriptions of his commentary contained herein. His roots and life experiences are quite evident throughout.

He considers himself a New Mexico native, although born in Utah, since he was conceived in New Mexico. His reverence for life is also obvious throughout the book.

He grew up in a middle class family with two working parents who daily shared growing up in the great depression. He learned the value of a dollar and the honor of work in any form.

Steve was admitted to medical school without an undergraduate degree at age 19 and graduated with honors from the University of New Mexico School of Medicine 35 years ago.

Eight years as Navy Medical doctor followed and then a return to New Mexico where for 28 years he has been a dynamic member of the medical community.

He has held most medical political offices as hospital chief of staff, county medical society president and state medical society president. He has served as a health consultant to Presidents, Senators, Congressmen, Governors and even the President of the AMA.

As a New Mexico State Senator, "the Honorable" doctor still loves the one-on-one association he has with his patients and still sees new patients every week.

He prides himself in marching to a different drummer than many traditional doctors. Thousands of people around the world attend his sold out lectures on how to care for these marvelous bodies we have the honor to live in.

Now he has finally put on paper the wisdom he shares with all who will listen. He describes this book as perfect for the baby boomer with ADD who doesn't want to put on their reading glasses. The concise chapters are filled with pearls for health.

PUBLIC ELECTED OFFICE:

2001-2008 New Mexico State Senator, District 9

Senate Judiciary Committee 2001-2004

Senate Public Affairs Committee 2001-present

Senate Rules Committee 2005- present

Legislative Health and Human Services
Interim Committee

EDUCATION:

Undergraduate: 1963-1966
University of New Mexico

Medicine: 1966-1970 M. D.
University of New Mexico
School of Medicine

1970-1971 Rotating -O- Intern
Naval Regional Medical Center,
San Diego, Ca.

1971-1974 OB-GYN Residency,
Naval Regional Medical Center
San Diego, Ca.

LICENSURE / CERTIFICATION:

Medical License:
New Mexico
California

Certification:
Diplomat American Board of
Obstetrics and Gynecology

Fellow of the American College of
Obstetrics and Gynecology

PROFESSIONAL ORGANIZATIONS:

American Medical Association

American College of Obstetrics & Gynecology

American Fertility Society

New Mexico Medical Society

Greater Albuquerque Medical Association.

PROFESSIONAL ACTIVITIES:

September 1969-May 1970
>   Physician District Clinic United Mission to
>   Nepal, Kathmandu, Nepal

July 1969-June 1977 Commander US Navy Medical Corps

July 1977-present Private Practice OB-GYN
>   Albuquerque, NM

January 1989-December 1989 Vice President
>   St. Joseph Healthcare Syst,
>   Albuquerque, N.M.

January 1987-September 1987 CEO Foundation Health
>   Plan

January 1995-2002 Associate Clinical Professor
>   UNM School of Medicine,
>   Department of OB-GYN

January 1996-97 President of Greater Albuquerque
>   Medical Association.

1997- 1998 Medical Director "Global Hilton" and
"Spirit of Peace" around the world balloon flights

March 2002-2003 President
New Mexico State Medical Society

2001-present: Internationally recognized lecturer on weight loss, health, nutrition and dietary prevention of disease. He is frequently seen on television and lectures monthly around the world. He has lectured on five continents.

2004-present International Teacher of Neonatal Resuscitation to medical school faculty and neonatologists around the world.

CAREER GOAL:

To teach the world that health lies not in the treatment of disease, but in the proper nourishment of our bodies and prevention of disease. To take this message around the world in order to relieve the pain and suffering and economic drain that illness has created, based chiefly on lack of nutrition, malnutrition, and unhealthy lifestyles.

To teach the people
of the world
that they were
"Born to be Healthy and Thin."